The BLESSING

Greg Powe

The Blessing
by Greg Powe

Printed in the United States *of* America
ISBN 1-931232-14-8

Xulon Press
344 Maple Ave. West, #302
Vienna, VA 22180
703-691-7595
XulonPress.com

Contents

Introduction

This book will start you on the path to realizing God's abundant provision and blessing for your life. As this teaching unfolds, you will learn principles from God's Word that will help you get what you need to live on this planet and do what He directs you to do. You will learn of God's abundance and splendor, and will see how to live within the promise of God for your life.

You have been blessed with God's blessing. No longer must you scrape and scrimp by, because the abundance of heaven is yours. No longer must you live a defeated life, because the promise of dominion is yours. No longer must you beg or borrow, because the bank of heaven is open for you.

I'm speaking from experience, because I used to be broke, broken, and hopeless. However, when I surrendered my life to Jesus Christ and began living the way God intended me to live from the beginning, my situation changed dramatically.

I'm going to show you the promise available to you as recorded in Deuteronomy 28:1-14 and other Scriptures, and how to walk in the blessing of God twenty-four hours a day, seven days a week. You'll become the kind of Christian you always wanted to be, but more important, you'll become the kind of Christian that God wants you to be!

I'm going to teach you about the importance of a relationship with God in this book, because the essence of the Christian relationship is closeness with Him. You'll see the importance of sitting at the feet of Jesus while the busy-ness of the world goes on around you.

Finally, I'll teach you the power of walking in victory every day. You will be as surprised as I was when you see how easy it is to be the head and not the tail. You'll wonder why you didn't see it sooner.

These principles aren't difficult, though they require change on your part. However, change is good if it leads you closer to God.

Take a moment to read what God has in store for you as you apply the teaching presented in this volume:

> *And it shall come to pass, if thou shalt hearken diligently unto the voice of the* LORD *thy God, to observe and to do all his commandments which I command thee this day, that the* LORD *thy God will set thee on high above all nations of the earth:*
>
> *And all these blessings shall come on thee, and overtake thee, if thou shalt hearken unto the voice of the* LORD *thy God.*
>
> *Blessed shalt thou be in the city, and blessed shalt thou be in the field.*
>
> *Blessed shall be the fruit of thy body, and the fruit of thy ground, and the fruit of thy cattle, the increase of thy kine, and the flocks of thy sheep.*
>
> *Blessed shall be thy basket and thy store.*
>
> *Blessed shalt thou be when thou comest in, and blessed shalt thou be when thou goest out.*
>
> *The* LORD *shall cause thine enemies that rise up against thee to be smitten before thy face: they shall come out against thee one way, and flee before thee seven ways.*
>
> *The* LORD *shall command the blessing upon thee in thy*

storehouses, and in all that thou settest thine hand unto; and he shall bless thee in the land which the LORD *thy* God *giveth thee.*

The LORD *shall establish thee an holy people unto himself, as he hath sworn unto thee, if thou shalt keep the commandments of the* LORD *thy* God, *and walk in his ways.*

And all people of the earth shall see that thou art called by the name of the LORD; *and they shall be afraid of thee.*

And the LORD *shall make thee plenteous in goods, in the fruit of thy body, and in the fruit of thy cattle, and in the fruit of thy ground, in the land which the* LORD *sware unto thy fathers to give thee.*

The LORD *shall open unto thee his good treasure, the heaven to give the rain unto thy land in his season, and to bless all the work of thine hand: and thou shalt lend unto many nations, and thou shalt not borrow.*

And the LORD *shall make thee the head, and not the tail; and thou shalt be above only, and thou shalt not be beneath; if that thou hearken unto the commandments of the* LORD *thy* God, *which* I *command thee this day, to observe and to do them:*

And thou shalt not go aside from any of the words which I *command thee this day, to the right hand, or to the left, to go after other gods to serve them.*

(Deuteronomy 28:1-14 KJV)

Stand on the Word of God, Christian, and see His mighty hand!

Part One

The Blessing

Therefore thou shalt love the LORD thy God, and keep his charge, and his statutes, and his judgments, and his commandments, alway.

And it shall come to pass, if ye shall hearken diligently unto my commandments which I command you this day, to love the LORD your God, and to serve him with all your heart and with all your soul, That I will give you the rain of your land in his due season, the first rain and the latter rain, that thou mayest gather in thy corn, and thy wine, and thine oil. And I will send grass in thy fields for thy cattle, that thou mayest eat and be full. Take heed to yourselves, that your heart be not deceived, and ye turn aside, and serve other gods, and worship them; And then the LORD's wrath be kindled against you, and he shut up the heaven, that there be no rain, and that the land yield not her fruit; and lest ye perish quickly from off the good land which the LORD giveth you.

Behold, I set before you this day a blessing and a curse; A blessing, if ye obey the commandments of the LORD your God, which I command you this day: And a curse, if ye will not obey the commandments of the LORD your God, but turn aside out of the way which I command you this day, to go after other gods, which ye have not known.

(Deuteronomy 11:1,13-17,26-28)

Chapter 1

The Blessing—God's Promises Made Real

There was once a man who had two sons. The younger said to his father, "Father, I want right now what's coming to me."

So the father divided the property between them. It wasn't long before the younger son packed his bags and left for a distant country. There, undisciplined and dissipated, he wasted everything he had. After he had gone through all his money, there was a bad famine all through that country and he began to hurt. He signed on with a citizen there who assigned him to his fields to slop the pigs. He was so hungry he would have eaten the corncobs in the pig slop, but no one would give him any.

That brought him to his senses. He said, "All those farmhands working for my father sit down to three meals a day, and here I am starving to death. I'm going back to my father. I'll say to him, 'Father, I've sinned against God, I've sinned before you; I don't deserve to be called your son. Take me on as a hired hand.'" He got right up and went home to his father.

> *When he was still a long way off, his father saw him. His heart pounding, he ran out, embraced him, and kissed him. The son started his speech: "Father, I've sinned against God, I've sinned before you; I don't deserve to be called your son ever again."*
>
> *But the father wasn't listening. He was calling to the servants, "Quick. Bring a clean set of clothes and dress him. Put the family ring on his finger and sandals on his feet. Then get a grain-fed heifer and roast it. We're going to feast! We're going to have a wonderful time! My son is here—given up for dead and now alive! Given up for lost and now found!" And they began to have a wonderful time.*
>
> (Luke 15:9-24 The Message)

Like the young son in this story that Jesus told, we often impetuously decide to go another direction and try to make our way. We listen to the voice of the world instead of the voice of God, and make decisions that are not in our best interest. We listen to voices that compete with God's voice, and leave the promise of our destiny in search of a cheap counterfeit.

With eyes clouded to what is around us, we turn a deaf ear to the One who ensures our future, and turn instead to glitz and glamour that are empty and void of any lasting value. Instead of eating the meat of life that brings nourishment to our bones, we eat the cotton candy of deception that disappears in our mouth without satisfying our hunger.

What Does it Mean to be Blessed?

The prodigal son didn't realize what it meant to be blessed. To him, being blessed was having his own way with what his father gave to him. However, before long he realized that the things his father blessed him with would run out, and he would be left with nothing. In fact, he became so destitute that he resorted to feeding pigs! This once wealthy young man had lost it all.

Being blessed is not about things. Things have the appearance of blessing, but aren't the blessing at all. If things were the blessing, many people who profess no love for God would appear to be more blessed then the most devout, blessed Christian! It's not about things.

Being blessed is not about power. Power gives the impression to those around it that the one who wields it is blessed or anointed. If that were true and power is the blessing, then the most powerful man or woman on earth must be the most blessed. However, we know that isn't true either. It's not about power.

Being blessed is not about influence. Influence has often been touted as the secret to a full life. Having a lot of charisma or charm enables one to move in the highest levels of the social ladder, giving the impression of having great influence. But charm and charisma don't go very far without God, and they lead to despair. It's not about influence.

Then What is the Blessing?

The blessing is about being in a covenant with God. It's living in a realm of closeness with the Father that draws His best to you. The blessing is an endowment given by God to those who abide in His presence. The blessing is His anointing on your life that enables you to have things, wield power, and exercise influence. It's His plan to prosper you and bring you into a place of abundance and prosperity. The blessing is the root that brings forth the fruit of all that God has in store for you.

Abraham walked in a covenant with God (Genesis 12). Because of their covenant relationship, God blessed all that Abraham did to the point that even those around him were blessed, including Lot, who lost the fruit of blessing when he left Abraham (Genesis 13).

Think of it this way. If you plant an apple tree in your yard, it will grow to eventually produce apples. Every day, the tree draws nourishment up through its roots to feed the growth at the end of each branch and twig on the tree. Fruit is produced that ripens until it's ready to eat.

One can stand under the tree when the branches are full of fruit and can even benefit from the tree's fruitfulness. However, it doesn't mean that the person is fruitful. He is benefiting only from the tree, which is fruitful. See, the fruit is an end result of the health of the roots. If the roots are unhealthy, no fruit will be produced.

Likewise with the blessing. Houses, cars, money, position, influence, power and anointing all flow from the root, which is the blessing. They are the fruits of the blessing, not the blessing itself. Likewise, your being in covenant with God is the root of the blessing. All this is added to you as you seek first the Kingdom of God and His righteousness (Matthew 6:33).

The Blessing is Promised

God promises to fulfill His plan for your life as you live in accordance with His Word. Jesus is the key to this wonderful promise of blessing God has for you, and as you move into His domain, you will see the fruit of it.

God is truly awesome, but because our senses are dulled by the world, we only glimpse His awesomeness as we go about our daily affairs. However, God has more in store for us than living weak, defeated lives. He has prepared the blessing for us so that we will never lack in anything, as long as we walk in obedience to Him. No thing is greater than God's blessing, because it's not about things – it's His promise and presence in our lives.

Too often, Christians get confused and think of the blessing as a new car or a big house. While these are effects of the blessing, they fall far short of the blessing. They are the fruit, not the root. Remember, things decay, but God's blessing lasts forever. Likewise, what you have does not determine whether you are blessed. If that were so, you would cease being blessed if all the "stuff" were taken away. However, the blessing is eternal and not temporal. It is forever including now, not just now. Things are only for now.

Deuteronomy 11:13-17 states that as you walk in obedience to God, He begins to bless all the efforts of your hands and all that you touch. God suddenly moves into what you do and His presence ushers in the profound blessing that He promised. As you take hold of the finished work of Jesus and walk in obedience to His commands, Jesus moves in: "*If a man love me, he will keep my words: and my Father will love him, and we will come unto him, and make our abode with him*" (John 14:23).

God promises, with Jesus, to come and live with you as you love Him and keep his words or commands. When God is present, His blessing – the blessing – is there as well. You come into His presence and begin to reap the benefit of His abundance and power. No longer do you have to live in lack or despair – God is on the throne and you are His child!

God's Presence Ushers in the Blessing

To walk in God's blessing, you must first take hold of God's promise, realizing that His presence is an integral part of the blessing in your life. You can't survive without God's provision of air, water, and nourishment. Likewise, for His blessing to be upon your life, you must be in His presence.

Isaiah had a wonderful vision of the Lord while in His presence that changed his life forever:

> *In the year that king Uzziah died I saw also the Lord sitting upon a throne, high and lifted up, and his train filled the temple. Above it stood the seraphims: each one had six wings; with twain he covered his face, and with twain he covered his feet, and with twain he did fly. And one cried unto another, and said, Holy, holy, holy, is the* LORD *of hosts: the whole earth is full of his glory. And the posts of the door moved at the voice of him that cried, and the house was filled with smoke.*
>
> *Then said I, Woe is me! for I am undone; because I am a man of unclean lips, and I dwell in the midst of a people of unclean lips: for mine eyes have seen the King, the* LORD *of hosts.*
>
> (Isaiah 6:1-5)

When ushered into God's presence, we, like Isaiah, are instantly aware of His holiness and majesty. At the same time, we are aware of our unholiness and the sin that stains our person. Like Isaiah, we cry out and seek forgiveness and wholeness in the midst of our imperfection. God knows all about our past, present, and future, but Jesus has covered our sin:

> *Come now, and let us reason together, saith the* LORD: *though your sins be as scarlet, they shall be as white as snow; though they be red like crimson, they shall be as wool. If ye be willing and obedient, ye shall eat the good of the land: But if ye refuse and rebel, ye shall be devoured with the sword: for the mouth of the* LORD *hath spoken it.*
>
> (Isaiah 1:18-20)

God, in His faithfulness, answers our prayer of repentance and our sin is purged. Our advocate, Jesus Christ, shed His precious blood for our sin, so our cleanliness is not dependent upon what we do; it's dependent upon what Jesus has already done.

When we are in the presence of God's holiness and perfection, we see and receive the precious promises God has given us. Then, like Paul, we apprehend that which has apprehended us (Philippians 3:12), and the truth of God's blessing descends around us. Then, as we see the glory of God and witness His abundant forgiveness in our own lives, we determine to always walk this path. We heed God's command to ". . .*put away the evil of your doings from before mine eyes; cease to do evil;* Learn *to do well"* (Isaiah 1:16-17).

Blessing or Curse – You Decide

How do you want to live? Are you walking in the good of the land or are you walking in desolation? God's promise to bless is sure and sound, and He will not violate His Word. The key is continuing to walk in obedience to His Word and statutes.

The Lord calls you to come reason with Him and put your sins under the precious blood of Jesus. That cleansing causes you to become pure and white as snow on the inside. That purity is what enables you to walk in the blessing of God.

> *Behold, I set before you this day a blessing and a curse;* A *blessing, if ye obey the commandments of the* LORD *your God, which I command you this day:* And *a curse, if ye will not obey the commandments of the* LORD *your God, but turn aside out of the way which I command you this day, to go after other gods, which ye have not known.*
>
> (Deuteronomy 11:26-28)

The Lord sets before you every day a blessing or a curse. What choice will you make today? Are you willing to let God lead you into the land that flows with milk and honey, or are you going to stay out in the wilderness, separated from your destiny in God?

Notice that the Lord set a blessing, not blessings, before you. God also set a curse before you in the same manner. The curse isn't the devil's doing; it's God's. What are you withholding from God that needs to be put under the blood of Jesus? What are you leaving undone that must be done before you can live in the blessing?

You choose where you live – blessed or cursed. Disobedience causes you to turn out of the way of the blessing and move under the curse. God doesn't curse you, He simply leaves you alone and that's curse enough! God declares that if you obey Him, the blessing is yours; however, if you turn to the right or to the left, He stands aside and lets you go.

Because the precious blood of Jesus covers you, God can't curse you. You've been forgiven of all your sin, but you can move yourself into a curse by turning aside. If you move out of the way of the blessing, you thwart its purpose in your life and fail to walk into the destiny God has in store for you.

You will walk in the fullness of the blessing based on the value you place on it. Therefore, if you allow sin to rule your life, you put little value on what God has given you. You don't value the blessing if you . . .

- allow sin of any kind to remain in your life
- don't quickly repent of sin
- let others talk you into sinning
- are hindered in obeying God because of others.

The blessing is the actual presence of God on your life so sin must not reign in you. God's presence is precious and worth more than all of creation together, so treat it with great care and concern. You have the advantage in all situations when you are covered by God's presence. No one can get the upper hand on you if you walk in the presence of God.

The devil will come at you with tricks of all kinds to try to get you to forfeit the blessing. He'll seek to take it away through religion, riches, robbery, and rebellion so you must be on your guard.

Realize today that the blessing is a tangible presence. You have it, because you've been blessed with the blessing!

What Happened to the Prodigal Son?

Remember the young son at the beginning of this chapter? He was living in the lap of luxury but didn't realize it. All it took were some bad decisions for him to lose all that his father had given him.

However, the story doesn't end there. When the young man came home, his father met him on the road and welcomed him back with open arms. Yes, he made some stupid choices, and yes, he had squandered the fruit of his blessing, but his father restored him as a son.

You may have been like him and wasted a lot of years. You may have lost a fortune because of a life filled with unwise decisions. Nevertheless, you can be restored. God's economics are different than those of the world, and His numbers always add up. Determine today to turn away from the past and embrace the future. The blessing is yours – reach out and take it.

God's desire is to bless you. You step into the blessing He has prepared through your obedience to His commands, so stop moving out of the way of the blessing by disobeying Him. Obedience is the key to your blessing!

God's Promises The Blessing

Take these steps:

1. Keep God's perspective – things are not the blessing.
2. Move from your side to His side.
3. Leave Egypt (the world) and enter the Promised Land of blessing.
4. Hear and then do what God says; now.
5. Worship God and God alone.
6. Experience blessing beyond your efforts.
7. Reverse the curse and walk in the blessing.

But it shall come to pass, if thou wilt not hearken unto the voice of the LORD *thy* God, *to observe to do all his commandments and his statutes which I command thee this day; that all these curses shall come upon thee, and overtake thee:* Cursed *shalt thou be in the city, and cursed shalt thou be in the field.* Cursed *shall be thy basket and thy store.* Cursed *shall be the fruit of thy body, and the fruit of thy land, the increase of thy kine, and the flocks of thy sheep.* Cursed *shalt thou be when thou comest in, and cursed shalt thou be when thou goest out.* The LORD *shall send upon thee cursing, vexation, and rebuke, in all that thou settest thine hand unto for to do, until thou be destroyed, and until thou perish quickly; because of the wickedness of thy doings, whereby thou hast forsaken me.*

(Deuteronomy 28:15-20)

Chapter 2

Blessing or Curse—You Decide

Get outta my face!" Bob yelled. "You can't tell me what to do! This is a free country; I've got rights ya know!" Bob's supervisor shook his head in disbelief, wondering how someone with Bob's potential could throw it all away because of pride. He wondered if Bob understood that instruction and correction came with every job.

"Bob!" said the supervisor. "If you keep this up I'll have no other recourse except to fire you. Is that what you want?"

"No!" screamed Bob. "I just want you outta my face!"

Holding his gaze steady on Bob's eyes, the supervisor told him, "You have a choice Bob. Either calm down so I can show what needs to be done, or go home – for good."

Reluctantly, Bob settled down and listened to his supervisor. However, deep inside his mind he was thinking, "You just wait . . ."

Blessing or Curse Comes By Choice

Like Bob, we have a choice. We can decide every day how

we want to live – blessed or cursed. God has not placed us on this earth to do our own thing. We are here for a purpose, and must decide daily whether to use each day to fulfill God's purpose in our lives or go our own way. The Bible declares:

> *Behold, I set before you this day a blessing and a curse; A blessing, if ye obey the commandments of the* LORD *your God, which I command you this day: And a curse, if ye will not obey the commandments of the* LORD *your God, but turn aside out of the way which I command you this day, to go after other gods, which ye have not known.*
>
> (Deuteronomy 11:26-28)

Let me ask you some questions:

- Are you living a weak, defeated life?
- Are you struggling just to get by with no end in sight?
- Does it seem as if life is passing you by while others get all the good stuff?

If you answered "yes" to any of these questions, you may very well be living under a curse. Now remember, God doesn't put curses on you, they come by choosing not to live under God's blessing. As I stated before, if you aren't living in God's blessing, you're living in the curse.

The blessing of the Lord is His endowment of power on you for success and prosperity. This simply means that wherever you go and whatever you do, you are endowed with power from God to succeed and prosper. With God on your side, how can you fail (Romans 8:31)?

The problem is not that God refuses to bless. The problem is that you choose <u>not</u> to be blessed!

"*How do I choose not to be blessed?*" you ask. It's really very simple: you walk in disobedience, which inhibits the blessing and brings the curse.

Living outside of God's blessing means you live a life of lack and despair. Everything you try to do seems to falter or fail, your money always runs out before the bills are paid, your kids disobey and dishonor you, your spouse wonders why he or she married you, your friends abandon you, your dog may not even like you. It's not a great place to be. Trust me, I know.

Before I came to Jesus, I lived in despair all the time. I was always broke, my family life was a mess, I owed back child support, and my car was always breaking down. Life was hell. But then, Someone grabbed hold of me. You know, when Jesus comes into your life, things should change. If they don't, you had better check to see if you really invited Him in!

Satan's Plan vs. God's Plan

As I grew in discipleship, I came to learn some very important truths, one of which was that Satan had a plan for me in the same way God does. Too often, I would submit to Satan instead of submitting to God. Every time I went the wrong way, I moved out of the blessing and back into the curse.

It didn't take long for me to realize that something wasn't right. I was a Christian, I loved God, but I still had problems. It didn't make sense. Then I realized that someone wanted me to fail. Someone wanted me to live a life of lack and despair, and to be a weak, defeated Christian.

That someone was the devil. Of course he wanted me weak and defeated. Living that way, I'm not a threat to his kingdom. The good news is that God had a plan for my life, too.

Christian, it's time to look up and see who you are. When you turned your life over to Jesus, you became His. You are a member of His household and are no longer separated from

Him. Jesus is your elder brother (Romans 8:29), not some far-distant deity that cares little for your well-being.

Satan's plan is to steal, kill, and destroy: "*The thief does not come except to steal, and to kill, and to destroy*" (John 10:10a NKJV). Knowing that, why would you trust anything he says? The problem is, the world has been deceived for so long that the truth is hard to believe!

When you realize that you are in God's family and that you are a child of the King, you will begin to understand that everything He has is yours as well. What kind of earthly father would leave his child out of the blessing? Likewise, what child would be left out of the Heavenly Father's blessing?

> *For everyone who asks receives, and he who seeks finds, and to him who knocks it will be opened.* Or *what man is there among you who, if his son asks for bread, will give him a stone?* Or *if he asks for a fish, will he give him a serpent?* If *you then, being evil, know how to give good gifts to your children, how much more will your* Father *who is in heaven give good things to those who ask* Him!
>
> (Matthew 7:8-11 NKJV)

Satan is ruthless in his attack against you, and he will not stop attacking until the Lord casts him into the lake of fire (Revelation 20:10). However, be encouraged. The Lord is on your side and is beckoning you to stay near Him. In so doing, you will overcome the attack of the enemy and will emerge victorious.

Jesus said in John 10:10b, "I *am come that they might have life, and that they might have it more abundantly.*" This message is very clear. You are promised the abundant life of a child of the King! Jesus broke the curse of Adam's sin and returned you to the promise of the Garden of Eden.

Satan casts seeds of doubt. Is the soil of your soul fertile to receive these seeds and cause them to sprout and grow? If so, you stand in danger of living in curse and not blessing. Remember who your King is. Then you will find the strength and will power to resist Satan and the plan he has for your life.

Rebellion and Disobedience – Carriers of the Curse

Rebellion is found at the heart of evil. All one has to do is understand what happened in Heaven before the creation of the world to see how rebellion altered things.

> *How you are fallen from heaven,*
> O *Lucifer, son of the morning!*
> *How you are cut down to the ground,*
> *You who weakened the nations!*
> *For you have said in your heart:*
> *'I will ascend into heaven,*
> *I will exalt my throne above the stars of* God*;*
> *I will also sit on the mount of the congregation*
> *On the farthest sides of the north;*
> *I will ascend above the heights of the clouds,*
> *I will be like the* Most *High.'*
>
> (Isaiah 14:12-14 NKJV)

Lucifer, now known as Satan or the devil, was an archangel who was created perfect in all his ways: "*You were the seal of perfection, Full of wisdom and perfect in beauty. You were in* Eden*, the garden of God . . . You were perfect in your ways from the day you were created,* Till *iniquity was found in you*" (Ezekiel 28:12b-13a,15 NKJV). His status among the heavens was great, "*You were the anointed cherub who covers; I established you; You were on the holy mountain of* God*; You walked back and forth in the midst of fiery stones*" (Ezekiel 28:14 NKJV).

Now, this same angel has set his hand to destroy God's

perfect plan. This was seen in the way he deceived Eve in the Garden of Eden (Genesis 3) and in how he tempted Jesus in the wilderness (Mark 1; Luke 4). His plan is still the same: destroy the people of God. One weapon he uses effectively is that of rebellion. Remember Bob at the beginning of this chapter? His life was marked by rebellion. He rebelled against all authority, great and small, because he wanted to have his own way all the time.

When one is caught in the trap of a rebellious lifestyle, seeking self becomes the strongest urge. Everything he does is designed to benefit self and exalt self over others. This lonesome way of life becomes even more tragic when you consider the broken lives and severed relationships left in its wake. Can you imagine anything worse than being left totally to yourself without Jesus?

But this is only part of the curse. Remember, the blessing promises that you will be blessed . . .

- going in and coming out
- in basket and store
- because all you set your hand to will prosper
- in victory as your enemies flee from you.

If you are under the curse, the opposite of the blessing is your lot. You will be cursed . . .

- going in and coming out
- in basket and store
- because all you set your hand to will falter or fail
- in defeat as your enemies overcome you.

Satan still uses the age-old weapon of deceit to gain the upper hand. He isn't above lying to you to get you to do the wrong things. He'll make you think things are going just fine and that you couldn't be doing better. However, the truth shining on that lie will expose it quickly.

- Where are your kids at midnight?
- What kind of friends do they have?
- Are you within one paycheck of financial ruin?
- How are things at work?
- How are things between you and your spouse?

Don't believe the lie! Eve believed it and look what happened to her entire family. Her husband, Adam, was reduced to a laborer; they were evicted from paradise and sent to a desert; her son, Cain, killed her other son, Abel, because of jealousy. What has the lie done to you?

Rebellion is an attitude before it becomes a behavior. What happens when someone in authority tells you what to do? Do you:

- Resist openly or quietly, moving slow to show who is really in charge?
- Complain and moan, letting everyone around you know that you are being treated unfairly because you have to do what is expected of you?
- Become defiant and refuse to do what you're told?

America's idol is freedom. Yes, you read this correctly. It's freedom. Americans have ridden the horse of freedom until they've forgotten what it means and what it requires. Too often, we insist on protecting our rights while trampling on the rights of others. Too often, we rail against the establishment but push our personal agendas. Too often, we lift up freedom's banner, but hide the banner of responsibility so nobody can see it.

The lie is clear: Have your own way. After all, you're like God. Isn't that the crux of what happened in the Garden? "*Do it your own way, Eve*," the serpent intoned. "*God doesn't know what He's doing anyway*." What must be remembered is this: When you take over God's seat, all the responsibility He carries comes your way as well.

Christian, it's time to pick up the torch of responsibility along with the torch of freedom. Embrace the truth and shun the lie. Accept responsibility for what you've done and seek forgiveness if necessary. As God told Job:

> *Who is this who darkens counsel*
> *By words without knowledge?*
> *Now prepare yourself like a man;*
> *I will question you, and you shall answer Me.*
>
> (Job 38:2-3 NKJV)

Knowing God Breaks Deception's Hold

You can learn a lot about the devil by watching the world. You can see the evil that is running rampant around the globe and know that a sinister mind is behind it. You can read the headlines about children killing children while parents stand by and blame music or the Internet. You can turn on your television set and bring the mess of the world right into your living room and be bathed in the slop of prime-time TV. Sex, violence, murder, and mayhem are served each evening as the choice morsels of America's toxic diet of "entertainment." But there is another way.

Jesus said, "*I am the way, the truth, and the life: no man cometh unto the Father, but by me*" (John 14:6). When you know Jesus, you know the truth. Salvation is an intensely personal event in your life. Jesus cuts through all the lies, all the facades, all the walls, and all the deceptive maneuvers to speak to your heart one on one. "You can run but you can't hide," the saying goes, and that's true with Jesus. Remember, the Holy Spirit has been drawing you and knows all there is to know about you.

It's interesting that God reconciled us to Himself before we reconciled ourselves to Him. Before we were even born, we were reconciled to God. All we have to do is accept the fact that God loves us and wants us to live with Him. This is a good thing, because God is not some pervert who just wants to take from you and give nothing in return. No! God wants to give you everything in exchange for your sin and despair. But He's not going to force you to love Him. In fact, He's even prepared a place for people to go who choose not to love Him or accept His love for them – it's called Hell.

You can learn what you need to know about God from His Word, the Bible. The Bible is a complete, infallible, inerrant book about God. It came from God, and so is completely true about God.

You get to know God by knowing His Word. It's all about a relationship. When God created Adam, He entered into a relationship with a creature far inferior to Himself. Yes, Adam was created in the image and likeness of God (Genesis 1:26-27), but he wasn't God. However, God chose to relate to Adam. Later, seeing that Adam was alone, God created Eve so that Adam and Eve could be companions for life.

This same benevolent God desires to have communion with you and me. We don't have to walk this earth alone and wonder where our next meal is coming from. We don't have to be in bondage to a life of sin and despair, wondering what happens when we die. God has answered all of these questions and more, and is looking for companions to share the answers with.

> [Jesus said] *Greater love has no one than this, than to lay down one's life for his friends. You are My friends if you do whatever I command you. No longer do I call you servants, for a servant does not know what his master is doing; but I have called you friends, for all things that I heard from My Father I have made known to you.*
>
> (John 15:13-15 NKJV)

John 1:14 declares, "*And the Word was made flesh, and dwelt among us, (and we beheld his glory, the glory as of the only begotten of the Father,) full of grace and truth.*" Jesus, the Word of God, lived and walked among people for thirty-three years. He was fully committed to the plan of the Father put in place before the foundation of the world. Jesus' commitment brings great comfort and peace to a lost and dying humanity. All we need to do is look to Jesus, the author and finisher of our faith, to see the mighty faith that motivated Him.

Therefore, we learn commitment by seeing the commitment of Jesus. As we grow in his likeness and stature, we become more and more like Him. Paul said in Ephesians 4:11-13:

> *And he gave some, apostles; and some, prophets; and some, evangelists; and some, pastors and teachers; For the perfecting of the saints, for the work of the ministry, for the edifying of the body of Christ: Till we all come in the unity of the faith, and of the knowledge of the Son of God, unto a perfect man, unto the measure of the stature of the fulness of Christ.*
>
> (Ephesians 4:11-13)

To grow into the stature of the fullness of Christ is an awesome thought. It becomes even more awesome when we realize that it happens at God's initiative and not ours. All we need to do is stay committed to the process and our growth is assured.

Get God's Word in your heart and in your mouth. As you do, you'll begin to see the mighty power of God displayed in your life and in the lives of those around you. God has designed you to succeed. He made success available to you so that you can be what God has called you to be.

How can you be the "head and not the tail" if you're a weak, defeated, broke, poor, failure of a Christian? You can't and you know it. Stop trying to rationalize your mess and get into the Word of God! You must be so in tune with Him that His Word is constantly on your mind and on your lips. Speak the Word, because it is life to your body and health to your soul (mind).

You Have the Ability of God Within You

The moment you received Jesus as your Savior and Lord, God's Holy Spirit took up residence inside of you. Immediately, you became a new creature and all the old stüff died. Paul wrote "*Therefore if any man be in Christ, he is a new creature: old things are passed away; behold, all things are become new*" (2 Corinthians 5:17). Notice that it doesn't say that the old man was cleaned up and given a new suit of clothes. No! Scripture says that "*old things are passed away*" and "*all things are become new!*" Take hold of this promise and begin to live the life God has promised you.

Set before you every day are both a blessing and a curse. What will you choose today? You have the power of God within you. You have been cleansed and washed with the precious blood of Jesus. You have the ability of heaven within your grasp. What will you choose?

The devil knows who you are. He knows that you are a child

of God and that the Holy Spirit lives inside of you. However, he also knows that your soul may still be in charge. If that's the case, his weapons of deceit and rebellion will cause you much pain and anguish. If you succumb to the lie and begin to rebel against God, you've automatically chosen the curse. However, if you choose the path of righteousness, you become blessed with the blessing.

Read this choice once again and then read about the blessing. I think that as you do, the decision will become a "no brainer" and you'll step off on the path to the blessing.

> *Behold, I set before you this day a blessing and a curse;* A *blessing, if ye obey the commandments of the* LORD *your* God, *which I command you this day:* And *a curse, if ye will not obey the commandments of the* LORD *your* God, *but turn aside out of the way which I command you this day, to go after other gods, which ye have not known.*
>
> (Deuteronomy 11:26-28)

> *And all these blessings shall come on thee, and overtake thee, if thou shalt hearken unto the voice of the* LORD *thy* God. Blessed *shalt thou be in the city, and blessed shalt thou be in the field.* Blessed *shall be the fruit of thy body, and the fruit of thy ground, and the fruit of thy cattle, the increase of thy kine, and the flocks of thy sheep.* Blessed *shall be thy basket and thy store.* Blessed *shalt thou be when thou comest in, and blessed shalt thou be when thou goest out. The* LORD *shall cause thine enemies that rise up against thee to be smitten before thy face: they shall come out against thee one way, and flee before thee seven ways.*
>
> (Deuteronomy 28:2-7)

What is your choice today? Will you be blessed with the blessing, or will you choose the curse?

Refuse to believe Satan's lie

Take these steps:

1. Hide God's Word in your heart.
2. Resist the devil and he will flee.
3. Believe the promises of God.
4. Apprehend the truth of God's Word.
5. Refuse to be enticed by Satan's trickery.
6. Look to the Author of your faith to guide you.
7. Choose the blessing instead of the curse.

Part Two

Keys to the Blessing

. . . God tested Abraham, and said to him, "Abraham! . . . *Take now your son, your only son* Isaac, *whom you love, and go to the land of* Moriah, *and offer him there as a burnt offering on one of the mountains of which* I *shall tell you."*

So *Abraham rose early in the morning and saddled his donkey, and took two of his young men with him, and* Isaac *his son; and he split the wood for the burnt offering, and arose and went to the place of which* God *had told him. Then on the third day Abraham . . . saw the place afar off . . .* So *Abraham took the wood of the burnt offering and laid it on* Isaac *his son; and he took the fire in his hand, and a knife, and the two of them went together.* But Isaac *spoke to Abraham his father and said . . .* "Look, *the fire and the wood, but where is the lamb for a burnt offering?"* And *Abraham said,* "My *son,* God *will provide for* Himself *the lamb for a burnt offering . . ."*

. . . Abraham built an altar... and he bound Isaac *his son and laid him on the altar . . .* And *Abraham stretched out his hand and took the knife to slay his son.*

(Genesis 22:1-10 NKJV)

Chapter 3

Keys to the Blessing #1—Obedience

Marcus was suspicious of everyone. All his life, people had taken advantage of him, and though he was only 15, he knew how to fend for himself. He learned early not to trust anyone and to rebel against any authority that challenged him.

Marcus lived in the poorest section of Baltimore, where everyone, it seemed, was either selling drugs or pimping prostitutes. Night after night, he would stand on the corner – his corner – and proffer his wares.

Fear of death was Marcus' constant companion, accompanied by the only thing he feared more – living like he lived. Marcus saw no way out and no way up.

Abdul had gone to school with Marcus, but now was in a new school with a unique program designed for people just like them. Here, the teachers were interested in their students and did all they could to help them succeed. Coupled with this was an incentive program offered to students who graduated from high school: free college tuition.

Marcus didn't believe there could be such a place as this.

His experience in school wasn't good, and he had been expelled so often that he was out more than in. The last time he had gone to school, he intended to confront his teacher because he made him stay late for talking in class. When a knife was discovered on him, he was arrested and was now awaiting trial.

What nobody knew was that Marcus truly wanted to succeed. He didn't like the way things had turned out and just wanted someone to be straight with him. Too often, he had seen teachers, the police, and others abuse their power and authority. Marcus only wanted the truth.

Could this really be true? Was there a place where even he could learn? Is it safe to hope?

Decisions, Decisions, Decisions

> *Multitudes, multitudes in the valley of decision: for the day of the* LORD *is near in the valley of decision.*
>
> (Joel 3:14)

Every day, we have decisions to make; choices confront us that promise either a blessing or a curse. Remember Deuteronomy 11:26: "*Behold, I set before you today a blessing and a curse.*" We have the responsibility of making these decisions and choosing the way we will go. Will we go along the path of blessing or will we choose the highway of curse?

It's very simple when you stand back and look at the big picture. Your choices really come down to these two: obey God or disobey God. Satan will cloud the issue until you don't know whether you are coming or going. But the choices are still the same; only the subject matter changes.

We often see in legal battles how attorneys seek to cloud

issues that are detrimental to their client's case and magnify issues that are in their favor. What is at stake can vary from a stern rebuke from the judge to fines levied for illegal behavior; from doing time in prison to the death penalty. Nevertheless, the question is really very simple: Did the person commit the act?

The story of Abraham shows clearly how we must live by the choices we make and either be blessed or cursed in the process.

God Made a Promise

God spoke to Abram when he lived in Ur. We don't know much about Abram before the account of his life begins in Genesis 12, but we do know that Ur was filled with idolatry, and pagan gods were worshiped with abandon. In fact, Ur was in the region of the world known as Babylonia, the seat of many pagan rituals and the center of ancient idol worship.

When God revealed Himself to Abram, He did so with a promise, thus beginning a lifelong friendship between God and His chosen servant.

> *Now the* LORD *had said unto Abram, Get thee out of thy country, and from thy kindred, and from thy father's house, unto a land that I will shew thee: And I will make of thee a great nation, and I will bless thee, and make thy name great; and thou shalt be a blessing: And I will bless them that bless thee, and curse him that curseth thee: and in thee shall all families of the earth be blessed.*
>
> (Genesis 12:1-3)

Notice the promise to make of Abram a "great nation" and that in him all the families of the earth would be blessed. This promise kept Abram and his wife Sarai going for many barren and fruitless years until the fulfillment of the promise was at hand.

What about you? Has God revealed Himself to you with a promise?

Often, God reveals Himself and we hear the promise, but because of the circumstances surrounding us, we fail to apprehend what God has said. Then, because of our unbelief, the promise slips through our fingers like so much running water.

Abram was promised a son. He clearly heard God and staked his future on the words of the Lord. However, time began to pass by. Year after year, nothing changed. Sarai was still barren and her biological clock was ticking. Did Abram really hear the Lord or was it only his deep desire and yearning for a son playing tricks on his mind?

Finally, Sarai could stand it no longer. She saw herself growing older and Abram becoming more advanced in years, and knew that naturally there was little hope of anything happening. Therefore, she decided to take things into her own hands.

> *. . . Sarai said to Abram, "See now, the Lord has restrained me from bearing children. Please, go in to my maid; perhaps I shall obtain children by her." And Abram heeded the voice of Sarai. Then Sarai, Abram's wife, took Hagar her maid, the Egyptian, and gave her to her husband Abram to be his wife, after Abram had dwelt ten years in the land of Canaan. So he went in to Hagar, and she conceived.*
>
> (Gen 16:2-4 NKJV)

Sarai would live to regret her decision to move ahead of God. In fact, so much tension developed between her and Hagar that conditions in the home became unbearable for both of them.

When we move out ahead of God and try to do things on our own, we are birthing Ishmaels. God gave Abram and Sarai the promise of a son; Hagar was not included. Disobedience often springs from our desire to move the hand of God instead of waiting for Him to move it Himself.

The Bible never promises the blessing for our own effort. However, the Bible does promise the blessing if we choose to obey and not turn from God. Every time we turn away from God and begin to follow our own ideas and agenda, we are serving another god besides Jehovah. The motive may be wonderful and the idea may be good, but is it God?

God's Promise Birthed Hope

The promise Abram and Sarai received gave them hope where there was none before. This promise, coupled with their strong desire to see it fulfilled, led them to try and make the promise come true themselves.

We do the same thing. Our situation may be different than theirs, but we attempt to fulfill the hope within us through means that are ungodly. Does this make us bad people? No! However, it makes us people who move ahead of God and into the danger zone of our own effort.

Thirteen years passed before God spoke to Abram again. During this encounter, God changed both his and Sarai's names to Abraham and Sarah. God also promised that Sarah would bear a son and that his name would be called Isaac. Later, the Lord appeared to both of them while on His way to Sodom and promised Isaac within the year. Finally, the son of promise would come.

Abraham believed God and out of his belief, faith grew. Abraham knew that God was trustworthy because of the way He had led him in the past. There was no reason to doubt what God would do because God had always held true to his promises. God promised Abraham:

- A new land
- A son
- Posterity more numerous than the stars.

> *When God made his promise to Abraham, he backed it to the hilt, putting his own reputation on the line. He said, "I promise that I'll bless you with everything I have—bless and bless and bless!" Abraham stuck it out and got everything that had been promised to him. When people make promises, they guarantee them by appeal to some authority above them so that if there is any question that they'll make good on the promise, the authority will back them up. When God wanted to guarantee his promises, he gave his word, a rock-solid guarantee—God can't break his word. And because his word cannot change, the promise is likewise unchangeable.*
>
> (Hebrews 6:13-18a The Message)

Hope causes us to set goals where we would set none before. Hope springs up within us and lifts our eyes to what can be, not what is. Hope compels us to believe, and believing builds our faith. See, it's hope that leads us straight into the arms of Jesus.

But what does all this have to do with obedience? What does hope have to offer that will cause you to obey rather than turn to your own way? You know just as well as I do that hope puts you on a different course.

God's promise is unbreakable and irrevocable. When God has put His name on it, it's as good as done. Numbers 23:19 declares, "*God is not a man, that he should lie; neither the son of man, that he should repent: hath he said, and shall he not do it? or hath he spoken, and shall he not make it good?"* One of the most important things we must learn as children of God is that He will follow through with what He says He will do. God is faithful; we are the unfaithful ones.

> *We who have run for our very lives to God have every reason to grab the promised hope with both hands and never let go. It's an unbreakable spiritual lifeline, reaching past all appearances right to the very presence of God where Jesus, running on ahead of us, has taken up his permanent post as high priest for us, in the order of Melchizedek.*
>
> (Hebrews 6:18b-20 The Message)

Taking hold of God's promise means that you've finally given up trying to do it yourself. You've tried it your way and found it didn't work, so now you give it to God and commit to doing it His way. You begin to follow God no matter how it looks or sounds, and you won't listen when people tell you there is another way.

If you believe the Bible and have chosen to accept it as God's Word, then it becomes God's *words* to you. Every time you read it, you become more and more settled in your heart.

What about the promises of God? Do you believe that God . . .

- sent His only Son to redeem you from death?

  For God so loved the world, that he gave his only begotten Son, that whosoever believeth in him should not perish, but have everlasting life.

  (John 3:16)

- promises you a reward in heaven for receiving Jesus as your Savior?

  In my Father's house are many mansions: if it were not so, I would have told you. I go to prepare a place for you.

  (John 14:2)

- sent His Spirit as a surety or deposit guaranteeing His Word?

  In whom ye also trusted, after that ye heard the word of truth, the gospel of your salvation: in whom also after that ye believed, ye were sealed with that holy Spirit of promise, which is the earnest of our inheritance until the redemption of the purchased possession, unto the praise of his glory.

  (Ephesians 1:13-14)

If you believe these promises, why not believe that God has promised the blessing to all who obey Him? Furthermore, why not believe that His promised blessing is for you?

Isaac – Abraham's Hope Fulfilled

Abraham stayed true to God's promise. Yes, he faltered in the beginning with Hagar, but when the promise was given a second time, he remained true to God's Word. Everyone must learn obedience. Scripture says that Jesus, "*though He was a Son . . . learned obedience by the things which He suffered*" (Hebrews 5:8 NKJV).

Abraham learned as he walked with God. He was not subject to the wrath of God because of his desire to learn the ways of the Almighty. Likewise, David, though an adulterer and murderer, pursued God's heart and found the forgiveness that God freely offers those who come to Him. It matters not what you've done, God will set you on the path of righteousness and will cover you with the precious blood of Jesus to cleanse you of all your sin.

Too often, we stand in judgment rather than reconciliation, and then watch as our brothers and sisters go down in flames. Do we trust God for our forgiveness and reconciliation? Then why not trust God for someone else to be restored?

Obedience is a righteous commandment of God. We are all held accountable for what we do and for whom we stand. Stand for Jesus and you'll not be disappointed.

When Isaac was born, Abraham and Sarah were very old. Naturally, there was no way for them to conceive and have a son. However, God promised and then stood firm on His word to fulfill that which He spoke to them.

Their hope was fulfilled in Isaac.

- They were promised a son; Isaac was he.
- They were promised a posterity more numerous than the stars of the sky or the sand on the seashore; Isaac fulfilled the promise.
- They were promised one to carry on the name and family lineage; Isaac was delivered to them.

Never give up on what God has promised you. It may come in your later years, long after your natural ability has expired. However, when that happens, it's all God. You can stand by and see the mighty hand of God move where you have no strength or power to move. You can see God do something that everyone else says is impossible, and then you can give Him the glory, honor, and praise for seeing it through.

Are you promised an Isaac? Are you promised something that only God can provide? If so, stand on the Word. Lean on God's arm and let Him bring it to pass. If you do, it will be far greater than anything you could have dreamed up yourself.

Abraham's Test

Isaac was Abraham's son of promise, but the test was just beginning.

God spoke to Abraham and told him to get ready to go on a journey. God wanted him to sacrifice his only son, Isaac, as a burnt offering. Abraham, filled with expectation and dread, I'm sure, arose early the next day and set out with Isaac and two servants. As they approached the place where God told him to go, he set out alone with only his son accompanying him.

Isaac was old enough to know how these sacrifices were to be done, and he knew that something was missing. That something was a lamb to be offered on the altar. However, having learned obedience from his father who had learned it from God, Isaac went with Abraham.

Finally, after setting the wood down and arranging it for the sacrifice, Isaac spoke. He asked Abraham where the animal was for the offering. Abraham, trusting God that He would provide, said, "*My son, God will provide himself a lamb for a burnt offering.*" *So they went both of them together* (Genesis 22:8). I like the way the King James Version translates this verse. It says that, "*God will provide Himself a lamb*" for the offering. We see this fulfilled in Jesus, the precious Lamb of God.

Abraham remembered God's promise to him about a son, descendents as numerous as the stars of the sky, and that all nations would be blessed through him. He knew that even if he did offer Isaac as a burnt offering, God would somehow raise him up and fulfill the promise made earlier.

God will not violate His Word, nor will He falter in fulfilling the promises He has made. Abraham knew that, so he stood on God's promise. He didn't have to remind God what the promise was, he just had to be obedient to what God required of him.

The entire crux of this teaching lies in the fact that Abraham was obedient, and not only Abraham, but Isaac as well. How do you think you can receive the blessings of God if you don't obey what He tells you to do? Jesus said that you are His friend if you do what He commands. Are you willing to obey?

The Blessing is Fulfilled in Obedience

We take hold of the blessing as we apprehend the truth of Deuteronomy 11:26-28. It's true, a blessing and a curse are set before us each and every day. What we choose determines our level of blessing. Are we dwelling in the secret place of the most High (Psalms 91:1), or do we live in the valley of decision, wondering which way to go?

It's important not to miss God. Standing in obedience is much better than falling in rebellion. God has set His hand to bless you. Are you ready to reach out and take what God has promised?

King Saul came to a point in his life where he chose to go the other way. His story is sad, because it didn't have to be this way.

God had commanded Saul to take the Israelite army and attack the Amalekites. Not only was he to attack, but the Lord also commanded him to utterly destroy them, sparing no person, animal, or thing. The army was successful, and the Amalekites were defeated. However, instead of doing what God commanded him to do, Saul allowed the king, Agag, to live, as well as the choice animals from their herds.

Samuel was grieved when he heard of Saul's disobedience, and spent the night crying out to the Lord (1 Samuel 15:10). Early the next morning, Samuel went to meet with Saul, finally catching up with him at Gilgal. When confronted, Saul made it sound like he had completely obeyed the Lord, and had done all that God commanded. However, Samuel knew what was in his heart.

When confronted again, Saul said it wasn't he at all, it was the men who were with him who refused to slay the animals. But again, Samuel pointed out his sin. Listen to what Samuel told Saul:

> *Samuel said, "Although you were once small in your own eyes, did you not become the head of the tribes of* Israel? *The* LORD *anointed you king over* Israel. *And he sent you on a mission, saying, 'Go and completely destroy those wicked people, the* Amalekites; *make war on them until you have wiped them out.' Why did you not obey the* LORD? *Why did you pounce on the plunder and do evil in the eyes of the* LORD?"
>
> (1 Samuel 15:17-19 NIV)

Saul was learning a lesson in obedience. Sadly, it was too late. God had already rejected him as king, and was grieved that He had chosen him.

Samuel was a man of honor, and was a man filled with himself. He had become so accustomed to being king that he forgot what it meant to follow. Saul is not unlike many Christians today. We do our own thing in the guise of following God and then wonder why God will not bless it! Saul said that the best of the land's livestock was brought back so that it could be sacrificed to God. The problem was, God didn't want it.

Saul didn't have a relationship with God. This can be seen in the way he addressed Samuel regarding the livestock: "*The soldiers took sheep and cattle from the plunder, the best of what was devoted to God, in order to sacrifice them to the* LORD *your God at Gilgal*" (1 Samuel 15:21 NIV). Notice that it wasn't "the Lord my God."

Saul didn't obey because he wasn't a friend of God.

Abraham obeyed because He and God were in a relationship. Saul would not be compelled to do anything, even if it were God Himself who told him to do it. Abraham obeyed out of love and covenant. Because of his obedience, Abraham was blessed far beyond anything he could have accomplished on his own. However, because of Saul's disobedience, he was rejected as king. Even what he did to "honor" God was rejected because of his rebellious and sinful nature.

> *But Samuel replied:*
> *"Does the* LORD *delight in burnt offerings and sacrifices*
> *as much as in obeying the voice of the* LORD*?*
> *To obey is better than sacrifice,*
> *and to heed is better than the fat of rams.*
> *For rebellion is like the sin of divination,*
> *and arrogance like the evil of idolatry.*
> *Because you have rejected the word of the* LORD*,*
> *he has rejected you as king."*
>
> (1 Samuel 15:22-23 NIV)

You cannot earn God's favor by what you produce. God's favor comes through obedience. The blessing comes when you have chosen to seek Him and not other gods. Yes, the promise is for you. You have set before you this day blessing or curse. Which will you choose? Will you serve God and be blessed, or will you chase an idol and be cursed? It's up to you.

Choose to obey God

Pray this prayer:

Father. I have decided to follow You because in You, and in You alone, I find completion and wholeness. You alone are worthy of my obedience, and so I commit to You today to serve and honor You. I choose a blessing, O Lord, not a curse. I choose to live in the palace of the King, and not the squalor of rebellion. You, O Lord, are my shield and buckler. You, O Lord, are the One to whom my allegiance belongs. Thank You, Lord, for leading me in the paths of Your righteousness. Amen.

Then the LORD *said to* Moses: "*How long will these people reject* Me? *And how long will they not believe* Me, *with all the signs which* I *have performed among them?* I *will strike them with the pestilence and disinherit them, and* I *will make of you a nation greater and mightier than they.*"

And Moses *said to the* LORD: "*Then the* Egyptians *will hear it, for by* Your *might* You *brought these people up from among them. . . .* And *now,* I *pray, let the power of my* LORD *be great, just as* You *have spoken, saying,* 'The LORD *is longsuffering and abundant in mercy, forgiving iniquity and transgression; but* He *by no means clears the guilty, visiting the iniquity of the fathers on the children to the third and fourth generation.*' Pardon *the iniquity of this people,* I *pray, according to the greatness of* Your *mercy, just as* You *have forgiven this people, from* Egypt *even until now.*

(Numbers 14:11-13, 17-19 NKJV)

Chapter 4

Keys to the Blessing #2—Prayer

Marie wept as she considered her plight. Every time she turned around, it seemed, she was in another mess.

"When will it end?" she cried. "Will I ever be free from all this?"

Robin and Samantha listened with understanding as Marie told of the latest tragedy to strike her. They looked at each other and knew that now was the time to begin praying in earnest for their friend. Though she had been reluctant to have them pray in the past, Marie was in dire straits now. So bad was the situation that only God could straighten it out.

"Marie," Robin said, "we have to call on the Lord to help with this problem. It's too big to overcome without Him. Will you join with Samantha and me as we pray?"

"Why would God help me?" Marie wailed. "I've never, ever given Him even a second thought. What makes you think He would help me?"

Samantha told Marie about the depth of God's love for her and how He waits until a person is willing and ready to accept

Jesus before He steps in. She also told Marie that their faith would join with hers and their prayer would rise to God as sweet-smelling incense.

"I don't have anything to lose." thought Marie. "Why not," she said. "What do I need to do?"

"Just believe." said Samantha. "God will do the rest."

God's Stealth Bomber

Weapons of stealth have proliferated over the past decade and now include many different types of aircraft, including bombers. Stealth technology renders these warplanes invisible to radar and makes it possible for them to deliver deadly payloads behind enemy lines.

The idea of stealth technology is to develop weapons that not only deliver crippling blows to the enemy, but also divert the potential of attack because of their existence. Saving lives is at the top of the priority list in the implementation of these weapons, and speedy conclusion to any armed conflict is a close second.

Christians have been using stealth technology for centuries and didn't even know it. We've been delivering crippling blows to the enemy by operating behind the lines cloaked in this secret weapon.

Sadly, many Christians don't know enough about this weapon, and so they are afraid to put it to use. Others don't know of its power and ability to deliver weapons of mass destruction to the enemy's camp and so leave it in the armory, depending instead on their own devices and schemes. Still others know of its power but only from a distance. Therefore, they choose not to use it because they don't feel qualified to sit at the controls of such a powerful weapon.

It's time to unleash this powerful stealth weapon and see

the mighty power of God released in your life. It's time to stop depending on your own strength and call in the reinforcements of God's army to deliver crippling blows to the enemy of your soul. It's time to move in close and see that as a Christian, you have the qualifications and skill at your disposal to do what God has called you to do.

So what is this mighty weapon of great power? Prayer! Yes, you read it right. Prayer.

Prayer is given to every believer as a tool and weapon of mass destruction. Jesus used it to disarm the enemy and make him a spectacle before the world (Colossians 2:15), and He taught the disciples how to pray so they, too, could gain the victory over the enemy.

When Jesus was ministering to the disciples at the Last Supper, He told Peter:

> *Simon, Simon! Indeed, Satan has asked for you, that he may sift you as wheat. But I have prayed for you, that your faith should not fail; and when you have returned to Me, strengthen your brethren.*
>
> (Luke 22:31-33 NKJV)

Jesus' prayer changed Peter's heart and set him on path that he would follow the rest of his life. Jesus' prayer led to Peter's victory, and when he returned, he strengthened his brothers indeed. In fact, Peter was crucified upside down to show his devotion to the Lord and his conviction that following Jesus Christ was the life to live.

How has your heart been changed because others have prayed for you? Nobody comes to the Lord in a vacuum, someone prays for everyone. The heavens rejoice when even one comes to saving knowledge of Jesus and accepts Him as Savior and Lord. Prayer is the weapon that brings the enemy to his knees and makes it possible for the Holy Spirit to minister salvation to a dying soul.

Mountains move because the powerful weapon of prayer has been unleashed on the obstacle standing in the way.

> *. . . Jesus answered and said to them, "Have faith in God. For assuredly, I say to you, whoever says to this mountain, 'Be removed and be cast into the sea,' and does not doubt in his heart, but believes that those things he says will come to pass, he will have whatever he says. Therefore I say to you, whatever things you ask when you pray, believe that you receive them, and you will have them."*
>
> (Mark 11:22-24 NKJV)

Often, we get caught in the crossfire between the proverbial rock and hard place, wondering where to turn and what to do. It's then that the Holy Spirit begins to rally the air force of mighty prayer within you to begin speaking to the mountain and commanding it to be removed.

The Power of Prayer

Once you understand the power of prayer, you'll appreciate anew the plan of God in your life and will mobilize the troops sooner rather than later. Prayer brings God into every situation you face. Then, with Him standing alongside you, the problem begins to diminish and the truth of God begins to grow within you.

Most Christians want to know that God's will is being done in their lives, and prayer is the tool He uses to show them. Prayer is the basic building block of a relationship with the Father through Jesus. Because it is foundational to walking in the depths of God's presence, it must be an integral part of every believer's life.

It's no different than building relationships with other people. If you don't talk with them or communicate in some way, a relationship is impossible. When you first meet someone and the relationship is in its infancy, you're drawn into closeness with him because of your desire to know him better.

Likewise, as you pursue your relationship with the Father, you are drawn into oneness with Him through spending time getting to know Him. James 4:8 declares, "*Draw near to God and He will draw near to you*" (NKJV). This promise is true and is made to all who seek to live in harmony with Him.

God will draw you to Himself. Jesus said in John 6:44, "*No one can come to Me unless the Father who sent Me draws him; and I will raise him up at the last day.*" As you are drawn to Him, you automatically lose yourself. When that happens, you become lost in Him and find that the Lord envelops your problems and weaknesses. Then, like Paul, you can say:

> *. . .He said to me, "My grace is sufficient for you, for My strength is made perfect in weakness." Therefore most gladly I will rather boast in my infirmities, that the power of Christ may rest upon me. Therefore I take pleasure in infirmities, in reproaches, in needs, in persecutions, in distresses, for Christ's sake. For when I am weak, then I am strong.*
>
> (2 Corinthians 12:9-10 NKJV)

Are you willing to cry out to God? Are you willing to let yourself go and seek the One who can move on your behalf?

Jabez Cried Out to God

> *And Jabez was more honourable than his brethren: and his mother called his name Jabez, saying, Because I bare him with sorrow.*

> *And Jabez called on* [cried out to] *the God of Israel, saying, Oh that thou wouldest bless me indeed, and enlarge my coast, and that thine hand might be with me, and that thou wouldest keep me from evil, that it may not grieve me! And God granted him that which he requested.*
>
> (1 Chronicles 4:9-11)

Jabez cried out to God and made his request known to Him. Learn to ask the Lord for what is on your heart. He is larger than any request you may make of Him and is ready and willing to meet your every need.

Notice that Jabez was *"more honourable than his brethren."* This follows exactly what we've been studying all along in this book. Deuteronomy 11:26 says that we have set before us each day a blessing or a curse. If one is honorable, he is choosing to follow the Lord and be blessed rather than follow the world and be cursed. Being honorable means more than just doing the right things; it's a way of life and an attitude of being.

Because of Jabez' beginning, he was known as one who brought pain and sorrow – that's what his name means. Simply having that name would be a constant reminder of pain and sorrow. Can you imagine going through life with a name that meant you brought sorrow? "*Hello, Sorrow. How are you doing today*?" Imagine that!

The key to Jabez' favor with God is the fact that he was more honorable then his brothers. In fact, he was so different that a genealogy was interrupted to insert the two verses that speak of him. He obviously stood head and shoulders above the rest.

Another fact of Jabez' favor with God is that he "cried out" to the Lord. When one cries out, it's more than just a simple "O *Lord will you help me*?" It's an urgent plea for mercy from the only One who could provide the mercy Jabez needed. "O *Lord*! I *need your mercy! Show me favor, O God, in all that I do."* Jabez cried out to the Lord.

God showed Jabez favor because of his faithfulness. Not only was he faithful in crying out to God, he was faithful in his obedience to God's commands. Because of his obedience, God heard him and showed him favor.

Moses Interceded for Israel

Moses, under the command of God, led the children of Israel out of Egypt toward the Promised Land. They had been slaves in Egypt for centuries, and were not experienced in self-government, nor did they have an organized form of worship.

Because of their immaturity and childish ways, they continued to rebel against God and His chosen servant, Moses. Their rebellious ways moved God to anger, and He even considered their destruction.

> *And the* LORD *said unto Moses, How long will this people provoke me? and how long will it be ere they believe me, for all the signs which I have shewed among them?*
>
> *I will smite them with the pestilence, and disinherit them, and will make of thee a greater nation and mightier than they.*
>
> (Numbers 14:11-12)

What makes this passage of Scripture so powerful is the heart of Moses! Instead of being lifted up with pride, he immediately began to intercede for the people. He could have agreed with the Lord and possibly lost everything because God may have been testing his heart. However, he chose the high road of integrity, and lifted the people before God in prayer: "*Pardon, I beseech thee, the iniquity of this people according unto the greatness of thy mercy, and as thou hast forgiven this people, from Egypt even until now*" (Numbers 14:19).

How would most people respond to this kind of situation? Would you choose to be exalted and have another nation spring from your loins, or would you stand in the gap for the people?

When you are looking for a body of believers to worship with, take a long look at the pastor. Is he willing to stand in the gap for the body?

Pastors have a great responsibility before the Lord. Not only are they responsible to Him for the safety of the "sheep" God has given them, they are also responsible for their teaching and discipleship. The prophet Amos explains how a shepherd will respond when the flock is threatened and the measures necessary to save it: "*Thus saith the* LORD; *As the shepherd taketh out of the mouth of the lion two legs, or a piece of an ear; so shall the children of Israel be taken out that dwell in Samaria*" (Amos 3:12a). The shepherd will not allow the lion to have even a piece of the ear of a lamb slain by the lion. Even if all that can be saved are two legs and a piece of the ear, the lion can't have it.

This is a perfect picture of Moses. He was so protective of the people God gave him that even when God was angry, Moses stood in the gap for them. His love for them was eclipsed by his love for the Lord, but he had God's love for them as well.

Hezekiah Cried Out to God

> *In those days was Hezekiah sick unto death. And the prophet Isaiah the son of Amoz came to him, and said unto him, Thus saith the* LORD, *Set thine house in order; for thou shalt die, and not live. Then he turned his face to the wall, and prayed unto the* LORD, *saying, I beseech thee, O* LORD, *remember now how I have walked before thee in truth and with a perfect heart, and have done that which is good in thy*

sight. And Hezekiah wept sore.

(2 Kings 20:1-3)

Hezekiah was a good king that did great things in the sight of God. However, as he began to prosper, pride entered into him and he began to pay more attention to the accumulation of wealth than the transfer of blessing upon the people of God. His house went out of order because he paid more attention to the effects of the blessing than he did the blessing.

Isaiah told Hezekiah to get his house in order because he was sick unto death. God, in His mercy, let him know it was serious and gave Hezekiah a chance to repent. Hezekiah cried out to God and began to pray, probably more earnestly than he ever prayed before.

Notice that Hezekiah didn't pray about the problems in his household or complain about how pride had turned his heart. Hezekiah repented and began to remind God of all the good things that he had done in obedience to God. The Bible says that the man's house was out of order, yet he turned to God and prayed. He didn't mention anything that was out of order; instead, he reminded God of how things were in order.

It's interesting that God immediately answered Hezekiah's prayer. Isaiah had only gotten to the courtyard when God spoke to him and told him to go back to the king.

And it came to pass, afore Isaiah was gone out into the middle court, that the word of the LORD came to him, saying, Turn again, and tell Hezekiah the captain of my people, Thus saith the LORD, the God of David thy father, I have heard thy prayer, I have seen thy tears: behold, I will heal thee: on the third day thou shalt go up unto the house of the LORD. And I will add unto thy days fifteen years.

(2 Kings 20:4-6)

God's desire is to see you blessed and prosper. Just like Hezekiah, cry out to the Lord and place your request before Him. James promises that when you do, God will not chastise you for asking (James 1:5), nor will He ignore you.

Hezekiah turned his heart toward God and chose the blessing instead of the curse. Prayer – fervent, sincere, and God-focused prayer – made the difference. This is an example of the effectual fervent prayer of a righteous man availing much. Hezekiah had a death sentence on him and God commuted it!

Notice that Isaiah didn't lay hands on Hezekiah, nor did Hezekiah make a show of standing before the nation. Instead, Hezekiah turned his face toward the wall and had a face-to-face conversation with God. Hezekiah knew that God was in a covenant with him and that he was in a covenant with God. Unlike a contract that can be broken or breached, a covenant lasts forever. Though Hezekiah had strayed from the covenant, it was still in place. All he had to do was move back in.

Prayer is Your Exchange for Blessing

Your countenance should always be one of either prayer or praise. In fact, prayer, praise, and worship are so integral with one another that it's difficult to separate them. Praise is a form of prayer because you're communicating with God the good things that are going on in your life. Praise is not murmuring or complaining; it's the exchange you make with God for the blessing. If you don't feel good, pray. How long should you pray? Until things change!

Prayer changes everything; it doesn't matter what's going on. If you have problems in your marriage, prayer will change your marriage. That's what changed mine. My wife prayed for me and didn't preach at me. One of the most useless things you can do is preach to an unbeliever to whom you're married.

Before you preach or try to expound the Word to them, or give them evidence of why they need to change, pray for them. Pray earnestly for them, night and day. Pray for them and let the Lord give you wisdom on how to minister to them.

There is power in prayer, and prayer is your exchange for the blessing. Prayer is one of the major exchange keys that God has given you for the blessing. If sickness attacks your body, make the exchange; if your finances are attacked, make the exchange; if your family is attacked, make the exchange; if your husband or wife is attacked, make the exchange. Don't just sit back wringing your hands and wondering what to do; now you know what to do – pray. Always pray and do not faint.

However, don't wait until things get bad to start praying. The most powerful prayer life involves a maintenance prayer program. In other words, don't drive into the ditch because you're praying to stay on the road. Every day, all during the day, pray and don't faint, lose heart, cave in, give up, or quit!

As you apply this key, you'll see mighty things happen in your life. All areas of your life will be blessed:

- Finances
- Health
- Relationships
- Spiritual Life.

Jesus didn't spend hours alone in prayer at night for nothing. He needed to stay in contact with His Father. All the great exploits of Jesus sprang from His prayer life. John wrote:

> *Jesus . . . said to them, "Most assuredly, I say to you, the Son can do nothing of* Himself, *but what* He *sees the* Father *do; for whatever* He *does, the* Son *also does in like manner.*

> *For the Father loves the Son, and shows Him all things that He Himself does; and He will show Him greater works than these, that you may marvel."*
>
> (John 5:19-20 NKJV)

Enter in through prayer. God will show you mighty exploits and will give you the strength and power to see them accomplished. **Use this key today to move into God's will and plan for your life.**

Move Out In Prayer

Take these steps:

1. Decide today to be a person of prayer.
2. Choose a quiet place to use as your "prayer closet."
3. Set aside time each day to spend in deliberate prayer.
4. Spend a few moments in quiet worship before beginning to pray.
5. Make your requests known to God; don't hold anything back. The Holy Spirit will help you pray as you should.
6. Expect to hear from God.
7. Believe that God will answer your prayers.

Even from the days of your fathers ye are gone away from mine ordinances, and have not kept them. Return unto me, and I will return unto you, saith the LORD *of hosts. But ye said, Wherein shall we return?*

Will a man rob God? Yet ye have robbed me. But ye say, Wherein have we robbed thee? In tithes and offerings.

Ye are cursed with a curse: for ye have robbed me, even this whole nation.

Bring ye all the tithes into the storehouse, that there may be meat in mine house, and prove me now herewith, saith the LORD *of hosts, if I will not open you the windows of heaven, and pour you out a blessing, that there shall not be room enough to receive it.*

And I will rebuke the devourer for your sakes, and he shall not destroy the fruits of your ground; neither shall your vine cast her fruit before the time in the field, saith the LORD *of hosts.*

And all nations shall call you blessed: for ye shall be a delightsome land, saith the LORD *of hosts.*

(Malachi 3:7-12)

Chapter 5

Keys to the Blessing #3—Tithing

"What is all this tithing stuff the pastor is telling us?" Brad asked. "I already give $25 a week! That's $100 a month! We could do a lot with $100 a month."

Stella knew that her husband, Joe, was struggling with tithing, but she just didn't know how much. "Pastor Jones just wants us to receive the blessings God has for us, Brad. It's a command from God and we need to take it seriously."

"But Stella," Brad replied. "I work all week to bring home $600. It doesn't go very far with four mouths to feed. Maybe Pastor Jones could kick in a few bucks to make things easier around here."

"Don't even go there, Brad. Maybe we aren't blessed because we're not being obedient to God. Pastor may be right. Maybe our money is cursed like he said today. He's been right about other things, you know."

"You're right, Stella. Maybe my attitude has been a problem too. Let's look at it again and see what we need to do to get our tithe done first, before anything else is spent."

Choose to tithe and Receive the Blessing

Many people are like Brad and Stella. They see what they have left after the bills are paid, and then wonder how they can ever afford to tithe. Too often, credit-card companies, auto loans, bank loans and other obligations prevent people from tithing. Sadly, they've bought into the lie that the tithe ended with the New Testament. The devil wants Christians to be broke, poor, bound to debt, and living from week to week, hand to mouth. He wants them to be powerless as they strive and work to pay off the "company store."

The tithe is still an important part of our Christian worship and stewardship. Nowhere in the Bible does it say that the tithe ended when Jesus rose from the grave and ascended on high. Yes, Jesus did fulfill the Law (Matthew 5:17), but tithing was instituted long before the Law was given! The idea that tithing has ended is nothing but bad theology for two important reasons.

1. Tithing was part of God's covenant with Abraham, which came *before* the Law of Moses. Therefore, it is not under the law.
2. Jesus redeemed us from the *curse* of the Law, but He did not redeem us from the blessing. Jesus came to establish and confirm the blessing. The Law still has blessings for us to receive.

Let's go back to Genesis to see the principle of the tithe with Abram. He tithed the plunder of successful warfare to Melchizedek .

> *And Melchizedek king of Salem brought forth bread and wine: and he was the priest of the most high God.*

And he blessed him, and said, Blessed be Abram of the most high God, possessor of heaven and earth:

And blessed be the most high God, which hath delivered thine enemies into thy hand. And he gave him tithes of all.

(Genesis 14:18-20)

Abram was faithful to the law of tithing, and God blessed him in both basket and store. One needs only to study the exploits of this great man of faith, known as the "friend of God," to see the hand of God at work in his life. No matter what he set his hand to, it prospered.

We are promised in Malachi 4 that as we honor the Lord in our tithes and offerings, we will walk in blessing. It follows the same pattern that we have seen in Deuteronomy 11:26. The Lord sets before us each day either a blessing or a curse; it's our choice.

Do you choose to be blessed or cursed? Obeying God's command to tithe means you choose to walk in blessing. Because many people have misinterpreted the issue of tithing, they forfeit the blessing of God. They think they can make things happen for themselves and so they don't need God's blessing. Therefore, they keep the tithe and seek to bless themselves with it. This is a dangerous misunderstanding, because when you don't tithe, you've made your choice, and you automatically fall under the curse.

Return to God and He Will Return to You

The Greek word, *dekatos*, means "tenth," and has also been translated as "tithe." Therefore, the tithe is one-tenth of your produce or income. We return to the Lord our tithe or 10 percent of that which we produce. It's returned to Him because it came from Him in the first place.

You can't out-give God. Therefore, give your tithes and

offerings in righteousness. Don't just give by the letter; give out of joy and thanksgiving. The promise of God is that He will provide for you because He is your source – not your job, your boss, or your family.

An exchange happens with tithing, so be careful not to miss it. You may think you have something, but really have nothing because it all belongs to God. Therefore, you must return to Him so He will return to you. You may think you're doing fine, but you don't know what fine is until you return to God.

Return unto God what is already His, and He will return something to you. If you don't, He will be prevented from returning to you what you need. Seedtime and harvest are much like inhaling and exhaling. If you want to continue living, you must keep making the exchange, inhale then exhale.

If your only desire is to receive and not give, you'll find that it doesn't work for long. Only receiving and not giving limits you, and keeps you from getting all that God has for you. Likewise, if you only inhale, your lungs fill to capacity and no more. Capacity doesn't increase beyond the size of your lungs, so the air you breathed in becomes stale and the life-giving oxygen inhaled is exhausted.

Many people want to only receive when it comes to their finances. They constantly seek to receive until they suffocate on their own selfish desires. They never give, so they are limited by their own self-imposed boundary. How much more God would give them if they would only open their hand to receive it! God's desire is to see His children blessed beyond measure. Our brains are too small to dream or conceive of all that God has in store. Our biggest problem is that we don't trust God to take care of our needs.

Will You Rob God?

Malachi 3:8 declares, "*Will a man rob God? Yet ye have robbed me.*" If I ask that question of you, what will you say? Will you ask, as the Israelites did, "*Wherein have we robbed thee?*"

God made it very clear to them that it was in tithes and offerings that they had so blatantly robbed the Lord. He showed them that they disobeyed Him for so long that they forgot what was required of them. They had done wrong for so long that they didn't know what was right anymore.

It's the same today. Statistics show that only a small percentage of Christians tithe. Sadly, they are in danger of forgetting the command of God. You can only disobey God for so long before you completely forget what is required in obedience to Him.

Often, people think that they can't afford to tithe. This view of life is so small and ungodly that it must be crushed and demolished from our way of thinking. How can one not afford to tithe? It's unthinkable to assume that God would have you return to Him what is His to the detriment of your finances. Isn't God bigger than your checkbook?

Jesus said that where your heart is, there will your treasure be as well (Matthew 6:21). So if you're worried about your money, if your heart is set on it, that is your treasure. What do you think about that? Isn't Jesus supposed to be your treasure? Jesus said:

> *Ask, and it shall be given you; seek, and ye shall find; knock, and it shall be opened unto you:*
>
> *For every one that asketh receiveth; and he that seeketh findeth; and to him that knocketh it shall be opened.*
>
> *Or what man is there of you, whom if his son ask bread, will he give him a stone?*
>
> *Or if he ask a fish, will he give him a serpent?*

> *If ye then, being evil, know how to give good gifts unto your children, how much more shall your Father which is in heaven give good things to them that ask him?*
>
> (Matthew 7:7-11)

Let me assure you, **you can't afford not to tithe!**

People often get legalistic in giving their tithe, but then neglect the offering, thinking that it's negotiable. Just as the tithe is not negotiable, neither is the offering. While the tithe is prescribed at 10%, the offering is up to you. One sure gauge to determine your love for the Lord is to look at the offerings you give. By the way, it's not just money. It includes all aspects of your life including your time, talents, and treasure.

God said to return unto Him and He will return unto you. What will God return to you? The blessing. He will return the endowment back unto you when you first return the tithe to Him.

"Prove Me" Says the Lord

> *Bring ye all the tithes into the storehouse, that there may be meat in mine house, and prove me now herewith, saith the* LORD *of hosts, if I will not open you the windows of heaven, and pour you out a blessing, that there shall not be room enough to receive it.*
>
> *And I will rebuke the devourer for your sakes, and he shall not destroy the fruits of your ground; neither shall your vine cast her fruit before the time in the field, saith the* LORD *of hosts.*
>
> *And all nations shall call you blessed: for ye shall be a delightsome land, saith the* LORD *of hosts.*
>
> (Malachi 3:10-12)

The Lord stated very clearly to "prove" Him in your tithes and offerings. This is the only place in Scripture where God says to put Him to the test and see His promise fulfilled. It's interesting that it relates to finances. Too often, paychecks are seen coming from the boss and the company is seen as the source of income. This tragic misconception is like deadly poison that destroys the muscles of faith.

Not recognizing God for who He is or what He does causes one to become cynical and bitter. One begins to view his paycheck as a debt that must be paid, and not as a gift from God. Bitterness and resentment begin to grow in the worker because his pay is never enough. Gratitude is replaced by ingratitude, and he is in danger of losing his perspective of God.

Change your attitude! God has given you all that you have, including the gifts, talents, and desire to do the very things you do to earn a living. Without God, you would be able to do nothing, and even the very air you breathe could be taken away. Your boss is not your source! God is. And God is much more concerned for you than an employer who sees you only as a means to an end (their success).

God tells you to prove Him. So do it! See if He is good to His Word. Begin by being obedient and see what starts to happen. God promised you wouldn't be able to hold the blessing that will come. Remember, if you can hold it in your hand, it's your seed, not your harvest.

God also promised to "rebuke" the devourer for your sake. Who is the devourer? Satan! His plan for you is to be poor, broke, starving, weak, and helpless. What better way to have it happen than to steal all your money? How much interest are you paying on your credit cards? It's the devourer. How much interest are you paying on your car, home, personal loans, etc.? It's the devourer. How much does it cost you to stay ahead of your neighbor and all his gadgets? It's the devourer. See, he's not your friend – he wants to steal as much of your money as he can to keep you under his usury thumb.

The word *rebuke* literally means, "to keep back." God promises that He will keep the devourer away because you're blessed with the blessing. God will keep him off you *"and he shall not destroy the fruits of your ground."*

Expand your thinking. Expect everything you touch to prosper. If someone walks past you on the street and touches you, expect them to be blessed. The Lord promised that your fruit would not be destroyed, and that He would rebuke the devourer for your sake. What was the exchange? Tithes and offerings.

Money Alone Doesn't Make You Wealthy

After Abram successfully rescued Lot (Genesis 14:14-24), he gave the plunder, less the tithe and provisions his men used, to the king of Sodom. He did this to demonstrate that it was the blessing of God that made him wealthy, not another man. Abram knew it was the exchange of faithfulness in the tithe that caused him to be blessed, and he knew that it wasn't about money or possessions. In fact, he knew that it wasn't the stuff that made him rich; it was the tithe, the exchange, and the blessing that made him rich.

Too many Christians try to get rich by accumulating great sums of money, large tracts of land, or expensive possessions. However, money doesn't make you wealthy. There are plenty of folks who are broke that have money. The problem is, they don't have the blessing, and are therefore living under a curse. Everything they set their hands to is devoured. They can't get ahead because they're cursed.

Consider Isaac

Genesis chapter 22 tells of Abraham's willingness to offer his only son Isaac unto the Lord. God honored Abraham's obedience and exchanged His only son, Jesus, so that we may have eternal life. What God does in the earth He does through men; that's His covenant law. Therefore, many people are still in the same condition of lack and despair because they have not honored God and obeyed His Word.

> *Then Isaac sowed in that land, and received in the same year an hundredfold: and the Lord blessed him. And the man waxed great, and went forward, and grew until he became very great: For he had possession of flocks, and possession of herds, and great store of servants: and the Philistines envied him.*
>
> (Genesis 26:12-14)

Isaac served the Lord and the Lord blessed him. The Philistines envied him because of his possessions, but it also went deeper. We often think that people are envious because of where we live or what we drive, but that's not it. People are jealous because we live in peace. We have peace in our homes, and our children aren't crazy or on drugs because we're blessed with the blessing of God. We're blessed going in and coming out, and we are the head in our homes and not the tail. The devil doesn't run our homes because Jesus is our Lord. People are envious because we have what they have or better, and we have peace with it as well.

Isaac learned from his father, Abraham, how to walk with God. Abraham took his role as a father seriously, and showed Isaac what it meant to be a man of honor and submission to the Lord. Though they were sojourners in the land, they were a family of great wealth. What the Philistines saw was a wealthy man, but God saw a man who honored Him and brought his first fruits to Him on a regular basis.

The Philistines saw that the Lord was with Isaac. Once you start walking in the blessing of God, people will see the difference between you and them. They will see the difference between someone who is cursed and someone who is blessed. Do people who tithe have a blessed look on their faces that non-tithers and God robbers don't?

God is With the Tither

God is with you when you tithe. He has to be if He's going to keep bad things from happening to you. Grace and mercy are at work on your behalf. Yes, you may have done things wrong and made some bad choices, but grace steps in and mercy shows up to deliver you from wrong decisions because you have the right heart.

Jesus said that where your heart is, your treasure will be there as well (Matthew 6:21). So set your heart in the right place and establish it with your seed. Therefore, even if you make a wrong decision, you can have confidence that God will not allow destruction to overtake you (Psalms 91).

> "*And, behold, I am with thee and will keep thee in all places whither thou goest, and will bring thee again into this land; for I will not leave thee, until I have done that which I have spoken to thee of*" (Genesis 28:15).

God promises to be with you and will stay with you till you see the manifestation of every word that He has spoken unto you.

Here is the exchange:

> ". . . *Jacob vowed a vow, saying, If God will be with me,*

> *and will keep me in this way that I go, and will give me bread to eat, and raiment to put on, So then I come again to my father's house in peace; then shall the Lord be my God: And this stone, which I have set for a pillar, shall be God's house: and of all that thou shalt give me I will surely give the tenth unto thee."*
>
> (Genesis 28:20-22)

Jacob told the Lord that on the basis of the promise of His presence, he would surely and without fail give a tenth, or tithe, of everything. That is the exchange.

Get it Right With God

If you have not been tithing, make the decision now to get connected to the blessing by making the exchange. Just get it right with God. Be like Jacob and return the tenth to the Lord. You cannot deny that God has been with you, and you'll find as you go through the Scriptures that there is an anointing released upon tithers.

The book of Malachi says you have a right to command some things. For example, you don't have to plead with God to protect your children. Instead, pray with boldness like this:

"*Lord, I'm a tither, and You have covenant with me, that great is the peace of my children. Lord, You said You'd keep the devourer away from my children so I'm standing on the promise You made.*"

God's promises are sure. He is the same yesterday, today, and forever, so the same promises He made with Abraham are yours today. One of the greatest struggles we face is in believing that God will do what He said He would do. Unlike most people, God is trustworthy.

I encourage you today to put God to the test. He promised that as you do, He'll be faithful and rebuke the devourer for your sake. Stand on His Word, and you'll get a view of life that is unsurpassed. Standing on His shoulders means that you are protected by His presence. His blessing surrounds you and your family, and His promise is as sure today as it was when He gave it. Listen to the promise of God as Brad and Stella did at the beginning of this chapter. Your response will energize His, and you'll see the truth of His Word.

Make the Exchange for God's Blessing With Your Tithe

Pray this prayer:

Lord, I stand on the promise of Your Word. You've promised that as I return to You the tithe, I could test You and see Your mighty hand at work. You promised to rebuke the devourer for my sake. Lord, I accept Your promise.

Thank You, Lord, for standing ready to bless me and my family. Strengthen me, I pray, that I may be a strong witness of Your provision and watch care. In Jesus' precious name I pray.

Amen.

Part Three

Living in God's Blessing

But where shall wisdom be found? and where is the place of understanding?

Man knoweth not the price thereof; neither is it found in the land of the living.

The depth saith, It is not in me: and the sea saith, It is not with me.

It cannot be gotten for gold, neither shall silver be weighed for the price thereof.

It cannot be valued with the gold of Ophir, with the precious onyx, or the sapphire.

The gold and the crystal cannot equal it: and the exchange of it shall not be for jewels of fine gold.

No mention shall be made of coral, or of pearls: for the price of wisdom is above rubies.

The topaz of Ethiopia shall not equal it, neither shall it be valued with pure gold.

(Job 28:12-19)

Chapter 6

The Effects of the Blessing

"I'll give $500 to the building fund if you'll let my grandson play his trumpet in church next Sunday," said Phil.

"It's all about money with him," thought Sam. "He always tries to get his way by throwing dollars around. Well, I'm not bending this time."

"No, Phil. The music has already been planned and the choir has been practicing for weeks in preparation. Maybe some other time."

Sam was disgusted with Phil's attitude. Yes, he has lots of money, but that doesn't mean he should be able to call all the shots. The problem is, Pastor seems to let him do what he wants for fear of losing his money.

"Sam, I'll call Pastor this afternoon to get this worked out," Phil said. "I'm sure he'll have something to say about it. You just don't see the big picture."

"There he goes again," thought Sam. "Now I'll have to rearrange everything and schedule the choir for another Sunday. This just isn't right. By the way he acts, you'd think he was the most important man on earth."

Things are not the Blessing

God wants His children to live in abundance. Remember that God placed Adam in a fully functioning and growing garden with everything he needed to sustain him and all the rest of creation. Adam was blessed, not because of all that he had, but because God provided everything for him. Don't mistake things like cars, houses, fine clothing, or social standing as the blessing. Things are <u>effects</u> of the blessing, not <u>the</u> blessing.

Too often, Christians pursue the wrong things, thinking that if they have this or that they're blessed. It's not stuff! If you have a relationship with Jesus, you're blessed. The effects of the blessing will follow getting blessed. It says in Mark 16 that signs follow those who believe. Notice it says <u>follow</u>. Things of the blessing follow the blessed. If they are in front of you, then you're following someone who's blessed and it's time you get blessed yourself!

Of course, some Christians don't have what God wants them to have because they are either ignorant of God's plan or they've been listening to the wrong people. Jesus is right: when the blind lead the blind, they both fall into the ditch.

Endowed With Power for Prosperity and Success

To be blessed is to be endowed with power for prosperity and success. You've been endowed with power, not endowed with things. Deuteronomy 8:18 declares, "*But thou shalt remember the* LORD *thy God: for it is he that giveth thee <u>power</u> to get wealth, that he may establish his covenant which he sware unto thy fathers, as it is this day.*" Once you have this endowment of power, you can get the wealth.

Possessions mean little if you are walking in God's blessing. It's common for things to work out for the blessed, just like it's common for things not to work for the cursed. If you see someone for whom nothing is working, you can most likely assume that they are not walking in the blessing.

Those Blessed are Endowed by God

To be endowed is to be equipped or supplied with a talent, an anointing, or a quality. Therefore, when you're endowed, you've been equipped. Do you have your equipment with you? Are you dressed for success? With the endowment of the Lord, you're equipped and dressed for success. This isn't about physical clothing; it's about having the anointing of God on you.

Adam was endowed with God's blessing while he was in the Garden of Eden. Because God's blessing was so evident in Adam's life, we can safely deduce that God's anointing covered him as well.

Many Christians are poor because they are in the habit of poverty thinking. They lose sight of God's view of things, and fall into the trap of thinking they are supposed to be poor. Christian, you don't have to live like a pauper. God's promise for you is prosperity, not poverty. So stop acting like you're poor, and quit poking around in the Word of God to find justification for having nothing. Begin thinking like an eagle instead, and get ready to soar.

Adam and Eve were covered by the endowment or blessing of the anointing of God. The glory of God literally covered them, and they were so completely clothed, they didn't know they were naked until they sinned. Only then did the glory of God lift and Adam was able to see both his and Eve's naked bodies.

Men and women have been listening to the lie of the serpent for more than 6,000 years. Because of this deception, more and more of God's glory has departed. The nakedness of Adam and Eve is increasing as we move further and further out of God's glory. We're further from thinking like God and from understanding what we've been endowed with. It's time for us to wake up and realize that it was God who dressed us. We've put on His blessing; we're clothed with Christ.

When you get up in the morning, look at yourself in the mirror and say, *"I'm clothed in God's blessing. I'm dressed for success."* Being clothed with God's blessing means you'll have unusual favor or an unusually favorable trait or anointing. All that you do will reflect the blessing of God, and the evidence of His favor will be plainly seen.

Exchanging Curse for Blessing

It is vitally important to first know how to get the blessing and then how to keep it. We can talk about the blessing and why we should be blessed, and we can discuss the increase in our lives that results from being blessed. However, just talking about it, but not knowing how to get it and keep it, makes it of no benefit.

To exchange means to give something in return for something received. As with anything of value, to receive the blessing requires an exchange. Often, people will try to receive the anointing or blessing of another person or ministry. They want God to bless them, but are unwilling to make an exchange for it.

Money is not the medium through which the exchange is made. Money may be used, but money itself is not the medium. Obedience is the medium of exchange that God requires. You can give all the money you have, but without obedience, it's of no value. God doesn't bless the good intentions of our heart. He blesses obedience.

The anointing cannot be bought or sold, as evidenced by this Scripture. More than once, people tried to purchase the power of God, not knowing that God could not be contained.

And when Simon saw that through laying on of the apostles' hands the Holy Ghost was given, he offered them money,

Saying, Give me also this power, that on whomsoever I lay hands, he may receive the Holy Ghost.

But Peter said unto him, Thy money perish with thee, because thou hast thought that the gift of God may be purchased with money.

(Acts 8:18-20)

Jesus told the disciples that they had freely received, so they must freely give. In the midst of that, there still must be a willing exchange.

The Bible says if you're willing and obedient, you shall eat the good of the land (Isaiah 1:19). You make an exchange for change. When you were saved, you didn't pay for it, but it cost you something. You had to change!

The Anointing is More than Method

You can't exchange something of no value for something of great value:

If it is an animal that men may bring as an offering to the LORD, *all that anyone gives to the* LORD *shall be holy.*

He shall not substitute it or exchange it, good for bad or bad for good; and if he at all exchanges animal for animal, then both it and the one exchanged for it shall be holy.

(Leviticus 27:9-10 NKJV)

Sadly, especially with money, people attempt to get something for nothing. Great value is placed on money in this culture, and it means everything to some people. However, if you want something more valuable than money, but are unwilling to exchange even value for it, you're not ready to change.

For example, if God tells you to give $1000 and you do so in obedience, you've exchanged that money through obedience for the blessing. The exchange is doing what God tells you to do, and it brings the blessing upon your life.

Watching others and mimicking what they do is not obedience. Even in the realm of tithes and offerings, don't just do what others do unless you are willingly obedient. Otherwise, God is not obligated to bless it, and you may just go broke doing it.

People often see obedience and then attempt to package it in a formula for receiving the anointing. It doesn't work, so don't try it. Methods do not bring increase in your life. The blessing is what brings increase.

Money can be a counterfeit blessing and expose a counterfeit anointing. A man with money can be deceived into thinking that he's anointed because he can have an effect. So long as the money holds out, he can cause things to happen. Nevertheless, when his money is gone, his anointing is gone as well. Phil and Sam at the beginning of this chapter illustrated this principle perfectly. Phil's money gave him the ability to affect or change the direction of worship. It had nothing to do with anointing and everything to do with a pastor who let money dictate the "movement" of God.

Remember, money is only one of the effects of the blessing, but it's not the blessing. If you limit yourself to only seeking money, you'll be seeking the lowest form of anointing. You can have power with money, but it is the lowest form of power, because when your money runs out, your power runs out, too.

Let me say it another way: money is influence. With money, you can influence things. There are people in this country that can influence elections with their money, but it's temporary. When the money is gone, their influence is gone.

Conversely, a person that's been clothed and endowed with

the blessing is secure. The money can run out, but they know how to get more. They aren't limited to the money in hand, because they're endowed.

You are Blessed and Endowed

When you are clothed with God's blessing, you'll walk in reverential fear of the Lord. That means walking in obedience to what God says. If you choose not to obey, then you will walk clothed with the curse. Fear of the Lord is wisdom and to depart from evil is understanding (Proverbs 1:7).

Walking in blessing means that you walk by faith, not by sight. The contract will come because you are blessed and endowed, not because your company's bigger, or because your accounting plan is complete. Don't misunderstand. You must be a good steward over what God has given you. If you're negligent, slothful, or lazy, you won't keep the blessing or the effects of the blessing flowing in your life.

People often talk about going into business for themselves, saying that the Lord gave them a plan. However, if one can't save two hundred dollars in two years, they aren't ready to go into business. If one doesn't have enough discipline to put resources back for funding of the plan that God gave, then how diligent will they be with the funds that come into the business?

You Must Deny Yourself

Jesus said in Matthew 16:24-26:

> *If any man will come after me, let him deny himself, and take up his cross, and follow me. For whosoever will save his life shall lose it; and whosoever will lose his life for my sake shall find it. for what is a man profited, if he shall gain the whole world, and lose his own soul? Or what shall a man give in exchange for his soul?*

Jesus was obviously talking about obedience. Denying yourself becomes a lifestyle, because self causes some of the biggest problems you face. Your self, your soul, doesn't want to change. It's where the root of selfishness resides, and it constantly wars against the spirit (Galatians 5:17).

Jesus asked what it profits a man to gain the entire world yet forfeit his life. What would you give as an exchange for a blessed life in the kingdom of God? What does it cost to make the exchange? The price is obedience, and if you're unwilling to pay it, you will not receive the blessing. What ever Jesus tells you to do, do it. He will not tell you to do something contrary to the Word of God.

Obey God With What You Have

Have you been limiting what God wants to do with you based on what you have? Isaiah 55:1 declares, "*Ho, every one that thirsteth, come ye to the waters, and he that hath no money; come ye, buy, and eat; yea, come, buy wine and milk without money and without price.*" How can you buy unless you have money? The only way you can is to be endowed! God is saying, "*Obey me with what you have, and I'll provide you with what I've declared is yours.*"

Isaiah 55:2 declares, " *Wherefore do ye spend money for that which is not bread? and your labour for that which satisfieth not? hearken diligently unto me, and eat ye that which is good, and let your soul delight itself in fatness.*"

You cannot solve spiritual problems using material things. People often think that money will solve their problems, but it won't. They . . .

- go to the mall and shop when feeling depressed
- try to boost low self-esteem by getting a new car.

The problem is, in a Lexus you're still nobody paying for a car you can't afford. That's materialism.

God wants you to listen to what He's telling you to do, and eat that which is good; let your soul delight itself in fatness. God simply said, *"Obey Me and you'll have more than you'll need. Obey Me and My Word, and you'll have more than enough."*

King Solomon is an example of one starting out blessed and finishing up cursed. The pattern of Solomon's demise is not unlike a lot of people and ministries we've recently seen. It's OK to have an abundance of things; just don't let the things have you. You must be careful, especially when God begins to increase your borders. Be careful listening to what people say and why they say it. The Bible says a wise man will hear and increase in learning. Just because you own a Benz doesn't mean you are any better than someone with a Dodge. Don't own anything as a status symbol; use it as a tool instead.

Don't Let Riches Unseat Wisdom

Solomon ascended to the throne after his father David passed away. He was young and was concerned with his lack of wisdom to lead the people, especially after seeing how popular King David was and how he led the kingdom.

Solomon was praying when God spoke to him and said He would grant anything Solomon desired. Pressed by the needs of the kingdom, Solomon said he wanted wisdom to lead the nation. God was moved by his request and granted it. He told Solomon that because of his selfless desire, He would bless him with wisdom like no other man before or since. Moreover, because Solomon didn't seek riches, God told him that he would be the wealthiest king of his day:

> *Behold, I have done according to thy words: lo, I have given thee a wise and an understanding heart; so that there was none like thee before thee, neither after thee shall any arise like unto thee.*
>
> *And I have also given thee that which thou hast not asked, both riches, and honour: so that there shall not be any among the kings like unto thee all thy days.*
>
> (1 Kings 3:12-13)

The Queen of Sheba came to visit Solomon, as recorded in I Kings 10, and was so impressed by all the wealth and prosperity that she wanted to be blessed like him. The queen saw the opulence of Solomon's court, and then made an exchange because she wanted what she saw on Solomon.

The queen said, "*Howbeit I believed not the words, until I came, and mine eyes had seen it: and, behold, the half was not told me: thy wisdom and prosperity exceedeth the fame which I heard*" (1 Kings 10:7). Notice the order, wisdom and then prosperity.

It didn't take long in Solomon's life for the order to switch – from wisdom and prosperity to prosperity and wisdom. After the Queen of Sheba left, kings from all nations began coming to visit and pay tribute to Solomon. Each visiting king brought great wealth to give to Solomon, so much so that when silver was given, it wasn't even counted. By today's standard, Solomon received in excess of $127,000,000 per year.

This is similar to the wealth of someone like Bill Gates of Microsoft. If he were to see a one-hundred dollar bill on the floor, it would cost him more in time to bend over and pick it up than to keep on moving – each of his minutes is worth about $600! And you thought there was a shortage of wealth.

Improper Handling of Wealth Can Upset Proper Order in Your Life

Solomon allowed things to get perverted and the end of his life is tragic. Beginning in I Kings chapter 11, we see his downfall unfolding. Verse one says, "*But king Solomon loved many strange women.*" Gentlemen, watch out for strange women. When the money comes in, strange women come around. It's the same with women. Ladies, when wisdom comes in, strange men show up. These strange women of Solomon led him astray to follow after the gods of their land. His heart became polluted with idol worship as he chased these women and their gods.

Riches replaced wisdom in the order of Solomon's life, and the order of priority was inverted. The end result of this inversion was that Solomon became perverted. God gave him wisdom and it produced riches, but he was so caught up with the riches that he put wisdom behind it all in his life. Wisdom was no longer the priority because money came first.

Solomon's problem was one of priorities. He was blinded by the gold and lost sight of wisdom. When he lost sight of wisdom, he lost sight of God. Remember, the fear of the Lord is wisdom.

Do you know when your priorities have been inverted? Do you know when you've allowed money to become the priority in your life and not wisdom? A sure test is when God tells you to make an exchange and you choose not to because you feel that money is more valuable than what God said to do. You've just told the Lord that the blessing is less valuable than your "hard-earned money." Your priorities have become inverted.

Set Your Priorities on the Lord

It's time to get your priorities straight. If your eyes are set on the glitter and glitz of gold and you've lost sight of the prudence of wisdom, turn around. You must realize that as you chase riches and not the blessing, you're going the wrong way.

It works like this. When you are anointed with the blessing, your eyes are on Jesus, not gold, and riches follow you; they pursue you. However, if you turn around and begin to chase after the riches, you are running away from the Lord. You are leaving the very source of your blessing behind. You'll never be able to catch the pot of gold at the end of the rainbow; it's always out of reach. If you don't turn back to the Lord, you'll live a life of frustration, lacking the very things that God has promised you in His Word.

It is God's will for you to be blessed. However, it's also God's will for you to learn how to handle the effects of the blessing: riches. You are called to be an overcomer, one who is not entangled by the entrapments of the enemy concerning wealth and prosperity. Therefore, when you live that kind of life, you will be able to finish strong and not pursue the false gods of the strange women or men who surround you.

God wants you to finish strong! He wants you at the front of the pack, leading them to victory!

The Effects of God's Blessing Follow You

Remember these points:

1. The blessing comes through your obedience and God's promise.
2. The blessing is not about things or possessions. It's about the Lord.
3. Things follow the blessing. You will be blessed materially.
4. Stay in touch with God. Don't let things take the place of Him.
5. Fear the Lord – it's the beginning of Wisdom.
6. Don't let riches pervert God's purpose in you. Stay focused.
7. Finish strong in the Lord.

For this commandment which I command you today is not too mysterious for you, nor is it far off. It is not in heaven, that you should say, 'Who will ascend into heaven for us and bring it to us, that we may hear it and do it?' Nor is it beyond the sea, that you should say, 'Who will go over the sea for us and bring it to us, that we may hear it and do it?' But the word is very near you, in your mouth and in your heart, that you may do it.

See, I have set before you today life and good, death and evil, in that I command you today to love the LORD *your God, to walk in* His *ways, and to keep* His *commandments,* His *statutes, and* His *judgments, that you may live and multiply; and the* LORD *your God will bless you . . .*

(Deuteronomy 30:11-16 NKJV)

Chapter 7

Walking in the Endowment of Blessing

Lester and Sylvia weren't convinced. Yes, they had heard the teaching and they wanted to believe, but something kept them from fully apprehending what the pastor was saying.

"How can we live like the pastor says we can live?" Sylvia asked. "We've never been able to get out of debt and stay out. I just don't see how it's possible."

Lester agreed. "How could we ever get a car or a house? For that matter, how could we even get a new television or stereo? I don't understand."

"I really want to believe," Sylvia said, "but I don't understand either. Pastor said that we could be the head and not the tail. He said that we would be the lenders and not the borrowers. Lester, don't you want to believe that, too? I don't want to be in debt for the rest of my life!"

"I don't either," Lester said. "Maybe we just need to begin believing in faith that what the pastor said is true."

God's Word is Near

Do you believe? Do you think that God has a plan for your life that includes an endowment of power to walk in His blessing? It's time to put aside all that you've been taught contrary to the Word of God and embrace His promise for your life.

You have read in this book many Scriptures that promise the blessing as you walk in obedience to God's Word. Sadly, many who read this still don't think the promises are for them! You must break out of the defeated, poverty-stricken mindset that has plagued you for years and get on with life!

God has a plan for you and He leaves nothing out of it. When I say that God has a plan, I mean that He has a plan for your life, including everything, your . . .

- Possessions
- Finances
- Relationships
- Household.

God's Word is near. He didn't deposit it where you can't find it, or make it so cryptic you can't understand what it means. God's Word is plain and simple, it's alive and ready for you to apprehend and make a part of your life. Read it, learn it, and make it yours. He sent it for that purpose.

You don't have to live in unbelief. God established His Word long before you were born. The principles in it are sure and time proven. Take it, it's yours.

You've been promised that if you choose to, you'll be blessed. You decide every day how to live: blessed or cursed. This principle is key to your understanding because <u>you</u> are the one who decides. Nobody can take God's promise away from you unless you willingly relinquish it. Likewise, you can take hold of God's promise and make it yours. Then you'll live in a state of blessedness that is unsurpassed by anything this world can offer.

Jesus frequently said, "He who has ears, let him hear." Do you have ears to hear the Lord? Have you tuned in to listen to what He says, or are you still listening to the junk the world has taught you? Remove those worldly tapes and plug in God's tape; your life will radically change and those around you will wonder what happened.

God's Word is plain:

> *See, I set before you today life and prosperity, death and destruction.*
>
> *For I command you today to love the* LORD *your God, to walk in his ways, and to keep his commands, decrees and laws; then you will live and increase, and the* LORD *your God will bless you in the land you are entering to possess.*
>
> (Deut 30:15-16 NIV)

Life and prosperity are set before you. Obey the command of God and you'll prosper. You'll walk in an endowment of power and blessing unlike anything you've ever experienced before. You just need to believe that God will do it.

God's Command is not Mysterious

So, what is God's command? What are you supposed to do to inherit all that God has for you? What does it mean to "walk in His ways"?

The Old Testament contains the complete Law of God that we call the Ten Commandments. Therefore, each time you see a reference to obeying the command or Law of God in the Old Testament, it referred to the Ten Commandments. However, Jesus was asked a question that helps shed light on what we're supposed to do.

One day, a teacher of the Law came to Jesus and asked Him what was the most important commandment. Jesus' reply was so simple yet profound that many who heard it (both then and now) thought it was too easy.

> *Then one of them, a lawyer, asked Him a question, testing Him, and saying, "Teacher, which is the great commandment in the law?" Jesus said to him, "'You shall love the* LORD *your God with all your heart, with all your soul, and with all your mind.' This is the first and great commandment. And the second is like it: 'You shall love your neighbor as yourself.' On these two commandments hang all the Law and the Prophets.'"*
>
> (Matthew 22:35-40 NKJV)

What can be more plain than this simple command to love? The teachers of the Law during Jesus' time interpreted the Law in such a way as to make it a burden to the people. Jesus resisted that, and instead interpreted the Law in a way that everyone could live. It's the law of love.

If you truly love someone, you will not harm them intentionally, nor will you lie, cheat, rob, or kill them. If you truly love someone, you'll not speak badly of them, nor will you assassinate their character. Gossip will not be on your lips when you speak in love, nor will you listen to it if someone else starts.

What Jesus was teaching is that love is the basis and foundation of all that we stand on. When love is the bedrock upon which relationships are built, they will not crumble, nor will they topple into the waves like those built on sand. Love is the mighty power that enabled Jesus to endure the cross and all that happened leading up to it. Were it not for love, we wouldn't have access into the Holy of Holies and the throne room of God.

Jesus paid it all, and love was what gave power to His precious blood, which was the currency used. Think for a moment about this awesome fact. Jesus said that Pilate could have no power over him unless it was given from above. Jesus laid His life down willingly and without reservation. This love-motivated act set the stage for the redemption of all humanity from the grip of death and destruction.

Love gives you the power to surrender your own will and embrace the will of another. Furthermore, when you embrace the will of another, you are still perfectly free. Your expression of love has relinquished your rights, yet the freedom that love brings to the act keeps you from being bound! This mystery of love is made clear in the way that Jesus went to the cross and suffered and died for us.

So, what does all this mean? It simply means that as you grow in your relationship with God, you will willingly relinquish your rights to Him. You'll experience freedom that you never knew you could, because you've completely placed your trust and destiny in His hands. You'll even find it's more difficult to be offended. Why? Because your identity is found in your destiny in Him, not in some tainted, worldly idea of who a man or woman is.

You can do this as you place your trust in Him and begin to love as He loves. You can love like Him because the Holy Spirit dwells inside of you; He'll teach you how. As you walk in His love, you will begin to understand the endowment of His blessing.

The Endowment of Blessing

One can see by the following definitions that an endowment comes from a source other than that which is endowed.

To endow is to:

1) furnish with an income

2) furnish with a dower
3) provide or equip gratuitously.[1]

An endowment is:
1) the act or process of endowing
2) something that is endowed
3) natural capacity, power, or ability.[2]

Using the third definition of each word, we can easily see that God is the One that provides (endows), and the provision (endowment) brings with it power or ability. The Holy Spirit guides and moves us to proper use of the endowment as we are daily led by Him.

Being endowed with the blessing brings great enjoyment, but at the same time great responsibility. Christians must realize that they are ambassadors of the Lord on earth (2 Corinthians 5:20), and when Jesus gives permission to use His name, great responsibility accompanies it (John 14:13-14).

The enjoyment you can expect comes from many directions but have the same source: God. You can expect blessings to come upon you and overtake you. You will be blessed in . . .

- the city and in the country (no matter where you live)
- coming in and going out (no matter where you go)
- basket and in store (you'll never go hungry or be without)
- the fruit of your womb (your children will prosper)
- the produce of your field (labor of your hands)
- everything you set your hand to (your business or job will flourish)
- victory over all your enemies (you'll not be overcome)

- your reputation among other people (you will be held in high regard).

God has prepared you to succeed. Not only that, He has prepared you to prosper. God has set His hand to bring abundance your way. Remember, abundance is "more than enough." In fact, God is going to increase your need so that He can bless you more than you think you need.

Here is a principle of abundance and blessing you need to know:

> *You view your needs based on what you see; what is before you. God views your needs according to* His *plan for your life; what is invisible to you. That is why God is always calling into being that which is not seen* (Romans 4:17). His *Word does not return to* Him *void, it accomplishes that for which it was sent* (*Isaiah* 55:11).

When you get hold of this truth, you'll see God move in ways that you only dreamed of before. More startling is the fact that you'll be right in the middle of it!

You are blessed to be a blessing. Yes, you will benefit from the blessing; however, the primary reason is to bless others. You will learn a principle that God has known from the beginning: when you bless others, when you give away what's in your hand, He can fill it with more.

Remember the fable about the dog and the bone? A dog had found a nice, big bone. He was on his way home and had to cross a bridge that went over a deep stream. As he was on the bridge, he looked over the side and saw another dog below with a nice, big bone. Selfishly, the dog snapped out with his teeth to get the bone from the other dog. When he did so, his bone dropped out of his mouth and fell into the depths. When the ripples subsided, he saw that the other dog had lost his bone, too!

What happened was the dog had seen his own reflection in the water and tried to grab his own bone, losing it in the process. Selfishness always results in the loss of what you have. Yes, you may hoard and have all kinds of possessions, but the joy of their use is gone. You are afraid to use them for fear of losing them.

Greed works in just the opposite way. As you try to take from others (including God) what is theirs, others are looking at what you have to try and steal it. Or, just like the dog, you open your hand to steal and are quickly stolen from.

It is much better to bless than to hoard. If you know who your source is, hoarding and greed are not problems to you. If you don't, then you may feel as if you will lose what possessions you have. This happens because you view yourself as the only source of what you have, and your resources are finite and exhaustible.

It's impossible to exhaust God's supply. His barns are always full, and His vats and cisterns always overflow with wine and water. The endowment of blessing is simply taking hold of what God has for you after making Him the focus of your life.

Choose Life and Good

Every day, God sets before you life and good. It's the blessing He sets before you. You can choose to walk in it or turn your back on Him and the blessing and walk in curse – the choice is yours.

What decision will you make today? Are you going to choose life or live in death? Here is the truth: You don't choose death; it's already on you until you choose Life (Jesus). See, you have the power to move away from the curse; just receive Jesus.

When Adam and Eve were in the Garden of Eden, God had

given them a command to refrain from eating fruit from the Tree of Knowledge. They chose to disobey God, and moved from the realm of life into the realm of death. The consequence, "you will surely die," is what happened. From that day until this, every human being is born unto death.

Because we are born unto death, we have little choice of how to live. It's unrealistic to expect anything from sinners except sin, so don't go there! However, Jesus came in the meridian of time to destroy death once and for all. His act of selfless love bought for every human being the opportunity to move into the realm of life. Death has been overcome, and you can benefit from the gift of God through Christ.

Jesus declared in John 6:44, "*No one can come to* Me *unless the Father who sent* Me *draws him; and* I *will raise him up at the last day*" (NKJV). The beauty of this passage is this: God desires all to come unto Him (2 Peter 3:9). Therefore, He is constantly drawing all persons unto Himself.

The problem is, people are rebellious and decide to turn away from the Giver of life, and therefore stay in a constant state of death. They are indeed the walking dead.

Our role in this life is manifold, including sharing the good news of life with everyone God brings our way. The worst thing you can do with the gifts God gives you is to hoard and to hide them away, so others can't participate with you in their enjoyment.

Do you know why God placed you here? To be a minister of reconciliation. Paul wrote in 2 Corinthians 5:18-19:

> *Now all things are of God, who has reconciled us to Himself through Jesus Christ, and has given us the ministry of reconciliation, that is, that God was in Christ reconciling the world to Himself, not imputing their trespasses to them, and has committed to us the word [ministry] of reconciliation.*

See, as you minister reconciliation, you are walking squarely in the middle of God's will and plan for your life. You are fulfilling the Law of Love that Jesus set forth, and therefore are being obedient to God's command. Guess what? You qualify for the blessing! You can step into the life God promised and lead others right in with you. What a blessing, indeed, to be the instrument God uses to bless someone in the most personal and dynamic way possible.

It's not hard, is it? Just reach out and take hold of God like He's taken hold of you. You will be empowered by the Holy Spirit, so there's no fear, and the reward is great. That's what walking in the endowment is all about.

Walking in the Endowment

Paul said:

> *Therefore, my beloved, as you have always obeyed, not as in my presence only, but now much more in my absence, work out your own salvation with fear and trembling; for it is God who works in you both to will and to do for* His *good pleasure.*
>
> (Philippians 2:12-13 NKJV)

To work out your salvation means to live it out or walk it out. Salvation is not a static condition; it's dynamic and living. Walking it out suggests that you don't find a groove and stay in it. Instead, it suggests that you plug into the Holy Spirit and let Him guide and move you. That means you will constantly be in a state of change, not scary change (though you may be challenged), but change nonetheless.

Walking in the endowment means living your life with God. When you wake up, the first thought on your mind is the Lord. When you go to sleep at night, the last thought on your mind is the Lord. No worrying, because you know Who your source is. No more despair or depression, because you know your destiny. No more failure or poverty, because you know Who your provider is.

When you know who you are, and have completely sold out to God, there is no fear! Boldness comes into your walk because you have no fear of falling or of failure. Why? Because the same Spirit that raised Jesus from the dead lives in you (Romans 8:11). If the Spirit that overcame death lives in you, then why in the world would you be afraid? It's nonsense.

Walking in the endowment is a journey of epic proportions. When Moses' mother placed him as a small baby in a wicker basket, little did she know that she was putting that baby into the hands of God to be used to deliver a nation.

When Jesse sent David out to tend the sheep, little did he know that he was preparing a king to reign. Nor did he know that he was fertilizing the soil of a young man's heart with time to spend in communion with God.

When Saul's mother looked at her little baby's face, little did she know that she held the most influential apostle of Jesus Christ in her hands. Nor did she know that out of his heart and mind would come the greater part of the New Testament, written by the Lord Himself through a willing vessel.

Look into the mirror. What effect will the blessing have on you? Sure, God may have given you some idea, but the fullness of it will not be visible until you can stand at the end and look back on it. God's idea is not to promote you for your sake. His idea is to promote you for His plan and purpose. Your need is small compared to what God sees your need to be.

> "For My *thoughts are not your thoughts,*
> *Nor are your ways* My *ways,*" *says the* LORD.

"For as the heavens are higher than the earth,
So are My ways higher than your ways,
And My thoughts than your thoughts."

(Isaiah 55:8-9 NKJV)

Take heart, Christian. God's desire for you is far greater than your finite mind can conceive and believe. God's plan is greater by far than any plan you can imagine for yourself. Remember, His mind and thoughts are far above yours.

Remember Lester and Sylvia? They were struggling with believing what God said in His Word. Whether or not they believe it does not justify or nullify the Word; it stands firm on solid ground. So what do you have to lose? Most people live in misery because of the condition of death they are constrained to. Why not take hold of God's Word today and make it yours? I promise you will not be disappointed.

Reach out today and take the hand of the One who can carry you there. He is much stronger than you and greater than any obstacle that confronts you. Choose life, and life will go with you wherever you go.

Walking in God's Endowment of Blessing

Remember these points:

1. God does not hide His Word from you, it's plain.
2. Learn to listen to the Lord and hear what He is saying.
3. Live by the Law of Love (Love God, love your neighbor).
4. You have the power of the Holy Spirit living in you.
5. There is no fear in the Lord, only boldness.
6. Your view of your needs is different than God's view – He has more for you to do.
7. Walk out your salvation daily and you'll walk in the blessing of God.

Epilogue

The road to the blessing is clearly marked. Thus far, we've examined seven signposts that point the way and direct us to our destination. Although we often try to make it complicated, it's not. God didn't design it that way, nor does He want us to fall into the devil's trap of thinking it is impossible to attain.

Let's briefly look at these signposts again to seal this teaching in our hearts and minds:

Signpost #1: The Blessing – God's Promise Made Real

God promises the blessing to all who obey His commands. The blessing is God's promise made tangibly real in the life of the believer. Scripture says that blessing will overtake you as a believer and will surround you. This expression of God's love is real, and your life as a blessed believer will show it.

Signpost #2: Blessing or Curse – You Decide

God sets before you each day a blessing or a curse (Deuteronomy 11:26-28). It's up to you, the believer, to decide every day whether you will live in a blessing or a curse. By choosing the blessing, you agree to keep God's commandments and thus shun the curse brought on by disobedience.

Signpost #3: Keys to the Blessing, #1 – Obedience

Obedience to God is of such vital importance that it is the first key to receiving the blessing. If you are not obedient, there is no further negotiation. The choice has been made and a curse is the result. However, as you choose to be obedient, the blessing follows and overtakes you. Jesus said the greatest commandment is to love the Lord God with all your heart, might, mind, and strength. The second is to love your neighbor as you love yourself. Living by the law of love ensures your qualification for the blessing.

Signpost #4: Keys to the Blessing, #2 – Prayer

Prayer is second only to obedience in importance. How can you expect to know the Father if you never talk with Him? The relationship must be developed and nurtured. That is done through communication, both listening and speaking. Being alone with God ensures that you'll learn the passion of His heart. You will discover His passion and then embrace it as your own, showing complete unity with the Father and demonstrating your desire to see His plan accomplished on earth. Flowing with His passion unlocks the blessing in your life.

Signpost #5: Keys to the Blessing, #3 – Tithing

Tithing is one area in which many Christians struggle. Often, they are so blinded by the enemy that they cannot see that by withholding the tithe, the blessing is withheld as well.

God's desire is to bless you so completely that your barns and storehouses are full. This means that you'll not be able to contain all that God wants to give you. Tithing opens the floodgates of heaven and carries forth the tide of blessing.

Signpost #6: Effects of the Blessing

Prosperity, abundance, wealth, and material possessions are all effects of the blessing. Prosperity means much more than material things. In fact, prosperity in God's definition means fullness in a relationship with Him. Therefore, an effect of the blessing is spiritual closeness with the Father and unity with His plan and purposes, not only in your life, but in the world as well.

Signpost #7: Walking in the Endowment of Blessing

When the blessing is bestowed upon you, the power of walking in it becomes real. Those who walk in the endowment of blessing walk in the power of the blessing. The power of the blessing means that fulfillment of Jesus' words is real today: *"Most assuredly, I say to you, he who believes in Me, the works that I do he will do also; and greater works than these he will do"* (John 14:12 NKJV). Signs and wonders will truly follow those who believe (Mark 16:17), and the blessing of God will rest on them.

You Can Choose

Joshua told the people to *"choose for yourselves this day whom you will serve . . ."* The same choice is yours today. Whom will you serve? God or mammon? Why not be like Joshua and say, "*But as for me and my household, we will serve the Lord*" (Joshua 24:15 NIV).

Endnotes

[1] "Webster's Ninth New Collegiate Dictionary," Merriam-Webster, Inc., 1983.

[2] Ibid.

9 781931 232142